I0814877

Vegan
Soulicious

Vegan Soulicious

PLANT-BASED ISLAND COOKING

Charlise Rookwood

PHOTOGRAPHY BY CLAY WILLIAMS
AND ANGIE VASQUEZ

ABRAMS, NEW YORK

Contents

11
INTRODUCTION

15
THE JOURNEY

19
SOULICIOUS INGREDIENTS

19
FROM MAURITIUS

23
FROM JAMAICA

24
INGREDIENTS FROM BOTH ISLANDS

27
VEGAN TOOL KIT

29
MY ESSENTIAL KITCHEN TOOLS

BREAKFAST

36
JAMAICAN "NO SALTFISH" FRITTERS

41
GREEN BANANA PORRIDGE

42
ACKEE AND "NO SALTFISH"

44
JAMAICAN FRIED DUMPLINGS

47
PLANTAIN BREAKFAST WAFFLE

48
BREAKFAST CEREAL SEA MOSS SHAKE

51
CACAO, SEA MOSS, AND MACA SMOOTHIE BOWL

52
TROPICAL CHARCOAL DETOX SMOOTHIE BOWL

55
SUPER FLUFFY "BACON" PANCAKES

58
TROPICAL PANCAKES WITH PAN-GRILLED PINEAPPLE

61
MANGO CHILE LASSI

62
JAMAICAN AVOCADO TOAST WITH FRIED PLANTAINS

65
COCONUT BROWN SUGAR RICE PUDDING

66
TROPICAL PLANTAIN AND "EGG" BREAKFAST SANDWICHES

MAINS

71
ROUGAILLE DIZEF (EGGS IN TOMATO SAUCE)

72
BOL RENVERSÉ (MAGIC BOWL)

75
GREEN CURRY WITH TOFU FISH, EGGPLANT, AND RICE CAKES

77
HOMEMADE IDLIS (SOFT RICE CAKES)

79
MINE FRIRE (MAURITIAN FRIED NOODLES)

80
ROUGAILLE SAUCISSE (SAUSAGES IN TOMATO SAUCE)

83
JERK MUSHROOM TACOS

84
GREEN BANANA RUNDOWN

87
TOFU VINDAYE

88
VEGAN FRIED CHICKEN

92
MAURITIAN LENTIL CREPES

95
VEGAN FISH AND CHIPS

98
BOUILLON CRESSON (WATERCRESS BROTH) WITH CRISPY LION'S MANE MUSHROOMS

100
TOUFFER HARICOTS VERTS ÀLA MAURICIENNE (SAUTÉED FRENCH BEANS WITH POTATOES)

101
MAURITIAN BUTTER BEAN SOUP

103
ONE-POT PUMPKIN SOUP

104
TOFU TIKKA KEBABS

107
NO SHRIMP CURRY

108
EAST LONDON KEBAB SHOP GYRO

111
EDGAR'S VEGAN GOULASH

SNACK TIME IN MAURITIUS AND JAMAICA: A STREET FOOD ADVENTURE

116
CRISPY ONION BHAJIS

119
GÂTEAU PIMENT (CHILE CAKES)

120
MAURITIAN GÂTEAU AROUILLE (TARO FRITTERS)

122
JAMAICAN VEGAN BEEF PUFFS

125
GRILLED JERK CORN ON THE COB

126
ROASTED AND FRIED BREADFRUIT WEDGES

129
FRIED BAKES

SIDE DISHES

133
ROUGAILLE SAUCE (TOMATO SAUCE)

134
ROUGAILLE PISTACHE (MAURITIAN PEANUT SAUCE)

137
VEGETABLE ACHARD (PICKLED VEGETABLES)

139
FRICASSER LENTILLES NOIRES (MAURITIAN BLACK LENTIL SOUP)

140
LISOU TOUFFÉ (MAURITIAN SAUTÉED CABBAGE)

141
CALLALOO SAUTÉ

142
JAMAICAN CABBAGE AND BACON

145
MAURITIAN CUCUMBER SALAD

146
HARICOTS ROUGES (SPICED RED KIDNEY BEANS) AND RICE

149
PILAU RICE

150
FRIED PLANTAINS

153
EFFORTLESS HOMEMADE CHAPATIS (INDIAN FLATBREAD)

155
SPICY BAKED OKRA FRIES

156
MARGOSE FRIRE (STIR-FRIED BITTER GOURD)

158
CHILE AND MAKRUT LIME GARLIC BREAD

159
THE CREAMIEST, CHEESIEST VEGAN MAC 'N' CHEESE—EVER!

DESSERTS

165
BRIOCHE BREAD PUDDING

166
DATE CANDY BAR

170
MAURITIAN TROPICAL FRUIT SALAD

173
COCONUT BANANA FRITTERS

174
LA DAUBE BANANE (SPICED SWEET AND STICKY PLANTAINS)

177
GÂTEAUX KOKO (MAURITIAN COCONUT MACAROONS)

178
MY FAMOUS THREE-INGREDIENT MANGO ICE CREAM

181
POUDINE MAÏS (POLENTA PUDDING)

182
STICKY TOFFEE PUDDING

185
MAURITIAN ALOUDAS (ROSE AND MINT ICE CREAM FLOATS)

ISLAND DRINKS

190
JAMAICAN GUINNESS PUNCH

191
CREOLE RUM PASSION COCKTAIL

191
TROPICAL SEA MOSS SLAMMER

193
JAMAICAN SORREL (HIBISCUS DRINK)

194
TAMARIND LEMONADE

TEA SOOTHES THE SOUL

198
GALANGAL BLOOD ORANGE TEA

200
GINGER TURMERIC TEA

201
JAMAICAN CHOCOLATE TEA

202
GRANDMA BERNICE'S JAMAICAN PINEAPPLE-SKIN TEA

FRESH JUICE

206
SWEET POTATO JUICE

207
SEA MOSS WATERMELON JUICE

210
UGO VERDE (GREEN JUICE)

211
CARROT JUICE

TIME FOR SOME SHOTS

214
LEMON ZINGER

214
APPLE CIDER VINEGAR SHOT

215
GOJI BERRY SHOT

215
BEET SHOT

VEGAN ISLAND PANTRY

219
TAMARIND SAUCE

220
SATINI COTOMILI (CILANTRO CHUTNEY)

221
PIMENT CRAZÉE (MAURITIAN CHILE GARLIC PASTE)

222
SATINI COCO (COCONUT CHUTNEY)

223
SATINI MANGUE VERT (GREEN MANGO CHUTNEY)

224
MANGO SATINI (MANGO CHUTNEY)

225
SCOTCH BONNET MANGO HOT SAUCE

226
CREAMY CASHEW-BASED TZATZIKI

227
KEBAB SHOP CHILI SAUCE

228
HOMEMADE COCONUT CONDENSED MILK

229
JERK DRY RUB SEASONING

231
HOMEMADE MAURITIAN CURRY POWDER

232
EGGY SEASONING MIX

233
ALL-PURPOSE SEASONING

234
KEEP PUSHING AGAINST THE FLOW

237
ACKNOWLEDGMENTS

244
PLANT-BASED ONLINE SHOPPING RECOMMENDATIONS

247
CELEBRATING COMMUNITY

249
MORE THAN AN APRON

250
INDEX

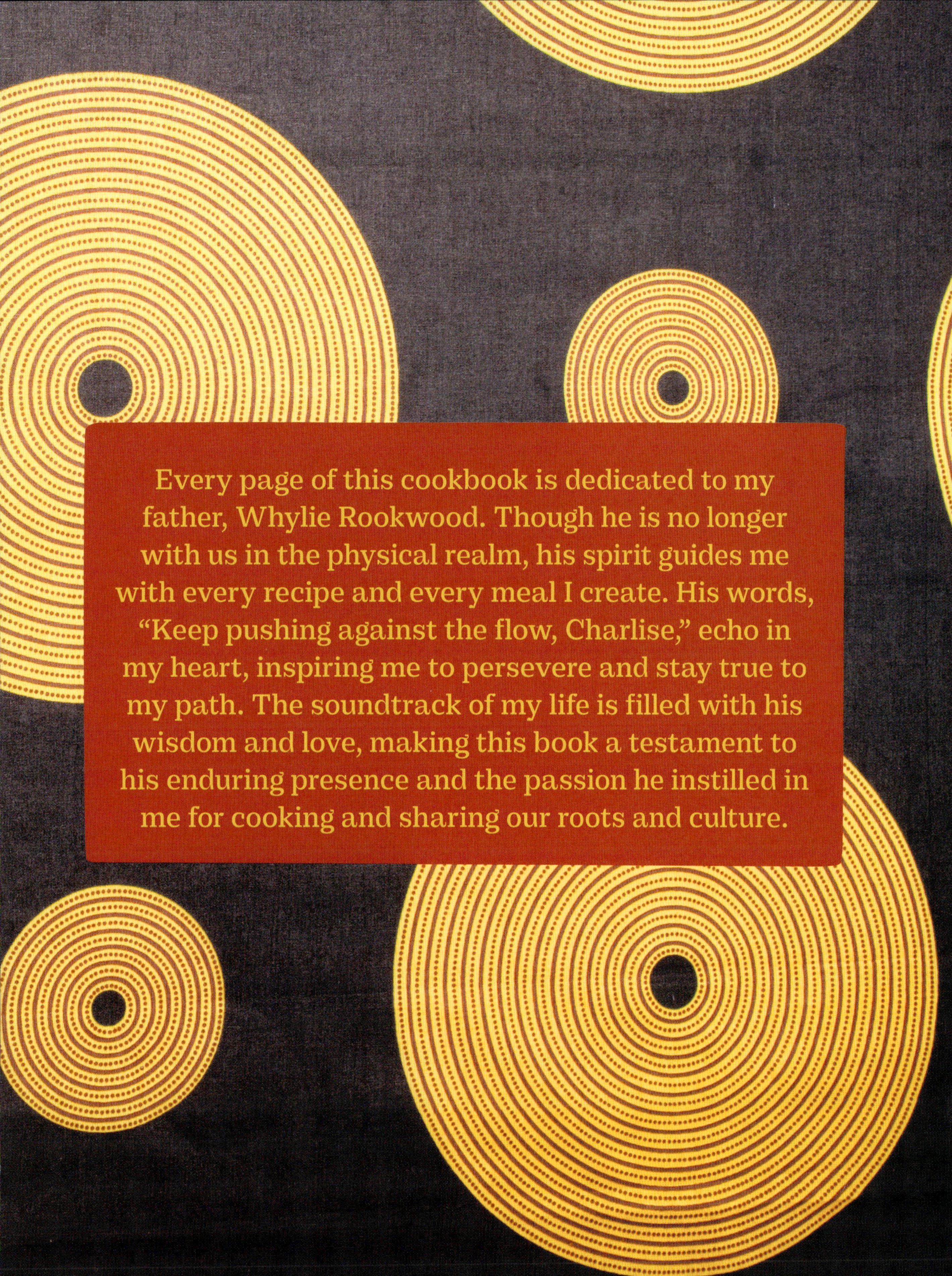

Every page of this cookbook is dedicated to my father, Whylie Rookwood. Though he is no longer with us in the physical realm, his spirit guides me with every recipe and every meal I create. His words, "Keep pushing against the flow, Charlise," echo in my heart, inspiring me to persevere and stay true to my path. The soundtrack of my life is filled with his wisdom and love, making this book a testament to his enduring presence and the passion he instilled in me for cooking and sharing our roots and culture.

I ♥ NY
ALL KIND SOUVENIRS

Introduction

My name is Charlise Rookwood. I'm an East London–born musician and self-made chef with Mauritian and Jamaican roots. Since going vegan and moving to the United States, I've been on a mission to create plant-based versions of my favorite childhood meals without compromising on flavor or comfort. I wanted to prove that, with a little love and the right seasoning, it's possible to bring all the vibrance and flair of island cooking to a plant-based lifestyle.

After developing dozens of plant-based recipes inspired by my Caribbean and African heritage, I created a platform called Vegan Soulicious to share them with my community and to raise awareness among parents and kids about healthier eating. During the pandemic – when we were all forced to stay indoors, cook for ourselves, and think about our health – I poured my life and soul into Vegan Soulicious's social media, determined to bring the joy of Mauritian and Jamaican food to as wide an audience as possible. I've since hosted my own cooking show, *The Black Vegan Cooking Show*, which was produced entirely by women and brought non-vegan celebrities – including New York rapper Jim Jones, comedian Donnell Rawlings, hip-hop royalty power couple Remy Ma and Papoose, and esteemed radio personality Angela Yee – into my kitchen to taste my cooking.

My recipes draw deeply from my family's culinary traditions. Although I've never lived in Mauritius or Jamaica, I frequently visited family in both countries during my childhood, keeping my connection with each culture alive.

My mother's family are Creole Mauritians. Mauritius is a French-speaking island nation in the Indian Ocean near Madagascar. Surrounded by the clearest blue seas and the whitest of sands, it's a tropical paradise where gorgeous fruits, vegetables, and spices grow in abundance. The island is so tiny you could drive around it in five hours, but it will likely take you double that time, because you'll want to stop so often to try all the street food and grab fresh mangoes right off the trees. Mauritian culture is built on a mixture of Indian, Chinese, African, and European influences. Thanks to this vibrant tapestry of cultures, you can get a huge variety of food on the island, but the best meals are the simple treats you'll find at the bustling Grand Baie Bazaar, where you can grab a dal puri (a flatbread stuffed with spicy split peas) and a fresh sugarcane juice for just a few rupees.

My dad was from Jamaica, and as a kid I spent a lot of time in the capital city, Kingston, where he was born and raised. In the mornings, my uncle Claude would often climb a tree and cut down a breadfruit to roast for breakfast – something I always looked forward to. My cousins and I would spend our days hiking in the vibrant green hills and exploring the fields, and we'd come home in the evenings to help our grandparents prepare dumplings. Jamaica's beaches are dotted with jerk huts grilling up the spicy, smoky meat the island is famous for. As you walk down the beach, you can see – and smell – their tall plumes of smoke from miles away, and you can hear reggae drifting from every radio and speaker. There's nothing better than cracking open a fresh coconut under Jamaica's blazing hot sun and drinking it so fast it pours down your face, or sitting down in the grass to devour a ripe jackfruit right where it landed from the tree.

In addition to visiting family in Mauritius and Jamaica, I was also part of a big Mauritian and Jamaican community while growing up in London; many members of my family had migrated to England in the 1950s and 1960s. Walking into an aunt's house for a party was like being transported to the islands, where every meal is a celebration of life and unity. And watching my immigrant grandparents and aunts prepare traditional dishes was my culinary apprenticeship – how I learned to create amazing family meals out of the simplest ingredients. In this cookbook, I'll show you how to do the same.

Welcome to the world of Vegan Soulicious, where I spill all my kitchen secrets and pour a whole lot of love and soul into each recipe. I'm a firm believer that cooking is not just about what's on the plate but about the vibes you bring to the kitchen. My family is full of musicians, so I can't cook in silence. For every recipe I make, I choose the perfect playlist, just as my dad would carefully select the perfect vinyl from his extensive collection before he cooked. See page 16 for a link to my playlist that I hope you'll listen to as you make the recipes in the pages to follow.

In this book, I've veganized some of the classic dishes from Jamaica and Mauritius, the homes of my ancestors. But make no mistake: my ancestors were rocking the whole plant-based thing way before it became a trend. Jamaican and Mauritian recipes naturally lend themselves to vegan interpretations; islanders eat from the land daily, except for the occasional fish or chicken. The plant-based life has been my playground since I was a kid!

My grand-mère on my mother's side was a Seventh-day Adventist, and therefore a vegetarian. During my childhood, I'd spend the weekends with her, and we'd cook vegetarian Creole Mauritian food together. My experiences cooking with her would become some of my biggest culinary influences. And many of my uncles are Rastafarians, pioneers of the Ital lifestyle, which is all about living purely, eating from the earth, and treating our bodies like the sacred spaces they are. Rastafarians adhere to a strict vegetarian diet because they believe that all living beings share a common energy from the Almighty. My family has been practicing this beautiful, natural way of eating since the 1930s. So, for me, living off the land and cherishing every bit of natural goodness isn't new – it's a legacy.

Now, let me tell you something about how we cook. In my family, measuring spoons and cups are more like suggestions than rules. We cook by feel, by taste, by the whispers of our ancestors guiding our hands, saying, "That's enough, child." It's a dance, a rhythm, a way to connect with generations past. Because I want you to be able to re-create these dishes and feel the same joy I do, I've translated this intuitive process into measurements and steps that you can follow easily. But

I promise, I've tried to keep the spirit of "just a sprinkle of this and a dash of that" alive in every recipe.

This cookbook is a journey through flavors and stories that have been passed down through the generations, now reinvented to celebrate the power of plant-based eating. From hearty stews and vibrant curries to refreshing drinks and sumptuous desserts, these dishes are my love letters to a heritage that flavors every bite with history and heart. As you flip through these pages, you'll get a glimpse into my kick-ass, soulful kitchen. So grab a spatula, pick a recipe, maybe dance a little while you're at it, and let's bring a slice of island paradise to your kitchen, one Vegan Soulicious meal at a time. Here's to good food, great vibes, and cooking that nourishes both your body and your soul!

The Journey

Food and music have always been the heartbeat of my life. They are the foundation upon which my world is built and the two elements that bring me the most joy. I grew up in a household rich in culture, surrounded by a fusion of Jamaican and Mauritian flavors and the sounds of the records my father played constantly in the kitchen.

My parents each migrated to rainy, gray London in the seventies from the beautiful, warm islands of Jamaica and Mauritius. It was a hard transition, but they crossed paths in this crowded city as teenagers. My mother was a model, and my father was a dancer and fashion designer. They quickly became a trendsetting couple, known in London for their flair, artistry, and dinner parties. They loved to entertain, and our door was always open to an eccentric cast of actors and musicians, including my uncle Bluey, leader of the world-famous band Incognito. My friends always wanted to spend time at my house, where there weren't many rules.

My parents' union was a melting pot of their cultures, and the food that came out of their kitchen embodied a spectacular marriage of flavors. Their connection would become the origin of Vegan Soulicious. By the time I was twelve, my father had me cooking Sunday dinner for the entire family. It was in that kitchen that I learned the importance of setting the mood – how the music you play can enhance the taste of food. He taught me that each ingredient brings its own unique melody, and, when you do it well, the flavors come together in perfect harmony. It was from him that I learned that cooking was not just about preparing food; it was an act of love, a way to connect, and a form of expression.

When I was eighteen, I hit the road and started touring as a singer-songwriter, and I signed with Universal Music Publishing. I spent the next twenty years in the music industry, but I never stopped cooking. It was a personal retreat from my fast-paced life, a chance to create, experiment, and reminisce. But after my father and three of his siblings all lost their battles with stomach cancer, I started to look at food in a new way – it reminded me of the intimate link between our health and what we eat.

When I became pregnant with my daughter, I knew it was time to make the change that had been brewing for years. I became vegan and never went back, and I made it my mission to transform the traditional dishes of my heritage into a symphony of vegan delights.

Don't forget the importance of setting the mood, both when you are cooking and when you are serving food to your friends and family. Here is a Vegan Soulicious-approved playlist to get you started.

Eight years ago, I moved to New York City with my then three-year-old daughter, and I quickly became disappointed with her school meals. So, I formed a plant-based after-school cooking class for first and second graders. I researched the diets of low-income students of color in the United States, and I saw an opportunity to help these communities eat healthy, plant-based meals without losing the flavors they enjoyed. The word spread, and soon I was supplying vegan baked goods to cafés across New York and New Jersey and taking on private catering jobs. Since the pandemic began, I've been sharing my recipes online, too, allowing me to reach a wide new audience. My recipes have resonated with millions of viewers across social media; the diverse influences and the home-cooked heart of island cooking make it relatable for people across the world. These are family-friendly dishes that kids love, too. My videos have gone viral and earned me the chance to appear on the *Today* show and to partner with brands. The success my recipes have found online shows how many people are eager to veganize their favorite comfort foods and expand their culinary horizons. They're starting to reimagine what's possible with plant-based meals.

But this cookbook isn't just a collection of recipes; it's a tribute to my father, who instilled in me the values of creativity, resilience, and the importance of feeding not just the stomach but the soul. I share these recipes infused with an abundance of love and light, in the hope that they do more than just satisfy your hunger. May they inspire you to embrace the joy of cooking intentionally healthy and nutritious food and to make every dish – no matter the occasion – as if your loved ones are right there, dining with you.

Because, in the end, we truly are what we eat. Let's embark on this delicious journey together and transform the way we think about vegan food – making it a soulful celebration of life, legacy, and culture. I'm here to bust some myths and show you that vegan food is so much more than eating salads every day. It's rich, it's hearty, it's flavorful, and it's deeply satisfying. From the sunny shores of Jamaica to the vibrant lands of Africa, I've gathered flavors and inspirations that I hope will show you the abundance that plant-based eating offers and make you fall in love with vegan food, just like I have.

CLOCKWISE FROM TOP: Curry leaves, green bananas, ginger, green chiles, Scotch bonnet peppers, scallions, Thai basil, thyme, garlic, plantain, tamarind, cactus, avocado, and eggplant

Soulicious Ingredients

My recipes are tied together with the enchanting flavors of key Mauritian and Jamaican ingredients—from fresh curry leaves and cardamom to chiles. These superstars elevate each dish and add a dose of goodness for the body and mind.

FROM MAURITIUS

Mauritian cooking draws from diverse global influences, including Indian, African, Chinese, and Creole cuisines. There are too many ingredients to mention here, but the following list includes key flavors you'll see crop up in many recipes in this book.

+ **CARDAMOM (WHOLE PODS AND GROUND)** This warm, aromatic spice fights harmful bacteria and helps build your immune system. It's peppery, floral, and citrusy.

+ **CHILES** Heat is everything in Mauritian cuisine. If you're not sweating at the dinner table, the meal isn't a success! Chiles are often added to curries, sauces, chutneys, and stir-fries to bring the heat, flavor, and depth. But beyond adding spice, chiles can improve your appetite, release feel-good endorphins, and increase your metabolism. For my recipes, I'll often simply call for a green or red chile. You can use the type of chiles you prefer depending on your spice tolerance and which are easy to find. Thai bird's-eye chiles (both fresh and dried) and jalapeños are good options and often readily available. For more on how to handle chiles and spice levels, see Scotch bonnet peppers (page 23).

+ **CILANTRO** Mauritian cuisine incorporates a lot of fresh cilantro. This peppery fresh herb comes from the lemon plant family and can help lower stress and anxiety.

- **CORIANDER SEEDS** These seeds from the cilantro plant are a fundamental component of Mauritian cuisine, known for their aromatic, citrusy, and slightly peppery taste. When toasted or ground, they release their flavorful oils, enhancing the depth and complexity of dishes like curries, stews, pickles, and spice blends.

- **CUMIN (WHOLE SEEDS AND GROUND)** This warm, earthy spice is often a key ingredient in curry blends. It adds depth and a slightly nutty, spicy taste to dishes.

- **CURRY LEAVES** You don't realize how important fresh curry leaves are to any curry until they're missing. They add a fresh, citrusy aroma similar to lemongrass and are full of fiber, calcium, and iron. Once you start using them, you'll never go back. I like to rub the leaves between my fingers to release their oils before cooking. But if you cannot find fresh curry leaves, it's fine to use dry ones.

- **FENUGREEK SEEDS** This tangy, bitter spice tastes like licorice and is prized for its ability to lower blood sugar.

- **GROUND TURMERIC** This spice has a warm, earthy, and slightly bitter taste with subtle hints of ginger and orange. It's commonly used in savory dishes, giving them a vibrant yellow color and a distinctive flavor. It also battles inflammation and can ease muscle soreness after exercise.

- **LENTILS/DAL** In Mauritian cuisine, lentils, particularly in the form of dal, hold a revered position, embodying a rich tapestry of flavors, cultural heritage, and nutritional value. These humble legumes are not just a staple ingredient but a cornerstone of Mauritian cooking, offering versatility, affordability, and a unique ability to enhance the taste and texture of dishes.

- **MUSTARD SEEDS** These seeds have a pungent, sharp flavor with a hint of heat. When toasted or cooked, they develop a nutty undertone. They are commonly used in pickling, spice blends, and cooking to add a distinctive tangy and slightly spicy taste to dishes.

To use the spices to their best effect, Mauritian cooks utilize the technique of tempering, and as you'll discover when you cook many of the Mauritian dishes in this book, it is a genius way to get the most out of your ingredients. Heating spices and other aromatic foods like chiles, garlic, ginger, and fresh herbs in hot oil releases their aromas, unlocks the health benefits of each ingredient, and infuses the oil with vibrant flavor and personality. Tempering is a technique that anyone who cooks Indian food will know well, and it is a game-changer for amping up flavor. You can either cook your food directly in the fragrant spices and oil, or you can add the oil to a cooked dish, like a chutney or a pot of cooked lentils, to flavor it. I'll walk you through the process in each recipe where this technique is used in the book, but there are a few general tips that can be helpful to keep in mind: When tempering spices, heat a neutral oil over high heat. I like to add a single ingredient like a mustard seed to see if it starts to sizzle, to ensure the oil is hot enough before adding the rest of the ingredients according to the recipe. You might want to quickly cover the pan when adding fresh curry leaves, as they will usually cause the oil to sputter. Don't walk away or take your eyes off the pan, as the spices can burn very quickly.

CLOCKWISE FROM TOP:
Sea moss, turmeric, black mustard seeds, cinnamon bark, cloves, salt, allspice, cardamom, cinnamon, coriander seeds, and maca root powder

FROM JAMAICA

Similar to Mauritian cooking, Jamaican cuisine is a fusion of flavors, spices, and cooking techniques influenced by many cultures. But where Mauritian cooking often starts with tempering spices, many Jamaican recipes begin with sautéing aromatics, including thyme, Scotch bonnet peppers, scallions, garlic, ginger, and yellow onions.

+ **ALLSPICE** This essential Jamaican spice, made from dried, unripe pimento berries, has a warm, sweet-spicy flavor profile with notes of cinnamon, nutmeg, and cloves. It's a key ingredient in both savory and sweet Jamaican recipes.

+ **CINNAMON, NUTMEG, AND CLOVES** You'll find this trio of spices in desserts and sweet drinks, like Jamaican Guinness Punch (page 190) and Carrot Juice (page 211). I call for both whole and ground versions of these spices. A spice grinder can come in handy!

+ **GINGER** The ginger in Jamaica is much more fiery and potent than the kind you'll find in the US. If you get the chance to pick some up from a Caribbean store, you'll immediately taste the difference. Ginger is like a miracle cure that can treat nausea, reduce inflammation, and elevate your mood. My recipes were developed using the regular ginger that you can find at any US grocer; some of them call for fresh ginger, but others make use of ginger paste that you can buy in a jar at most supermarkets. (I recommend the Shan brand for both ginger and garlic paste.) I tend to be generous with the quantity of ginger I call for in my recipes, since this flavor is so key to Jamaican cooking.

+ **PLANTAINS** This is a staple food in Jamaican culture, enjoyed in various forms such as fried, boiled, and roasted. Fried plantains are a common sweet-and-savory component of many Jamaican meals, but they also make an excellent side dish all on their own.

+ **SCOTCH BONNET PEPPERS** In Jamaican cuisine, there's only one kind of chile you'll ever need. Scotch bonnets are one of the hottest peppers in the world, approximately forty times hotter than a jalapeño, so use them sparingly! I recommend wearing gloves and washing your hands, cutting board, knife, and anything else the peppers touch immediately after handling them. Be mindful that the heat is primarily in the seeds and membrane of chiles, so I recommend removing these. You can substitute habaneros, which offer a similar level of spice, if Scotch bonnets are unavailable. If you prefer no heat, skip the chile altogether. Try fresh red Thai (bird's-eye) chiles for a medium-hot option. If you want a milder pepper, try a jalapeño.

+ **SEA MOSS** Jamaicans traditionally consume fresh sea moss gel on its own to boost energy and vitality just like you'd take a daily vitamin. In this cookbook, you'll find it in a variety of smoothies and shakes as a practically tasteless and therefore versatile supplement!

+ **THYME** This is a familiar herb in the US, but unlike at American grocery stores, markets in Jamaica will offer many kinds of thyme. More than a hundred varieties grow on the island! Don't worry, though, you can still achieve signature Jamaican flavors for the recipes in this book with whatever kind is available at your market.

INGREDIENTS FROM BOTH ISLANDS

In my family, we've noticed that Mauritius and Jamaica share a number of similarities when it comes to cooking. The two islands may have their differences in cuisine and culture, but the ingredients below are important components for both kinds of cooking. Meals in my family blend these shared elements and our own unique touches, creating a beautiful fusion of flavors and traditions that brings us together.

+ COCONUT The only oil my Jamaican family has ever used in cooking is coconut oil. It has a high smoke point, meaning that you can heat it to high temperatures quickly without it burning. It's great to have a tub of coconut oil around the house because, outside of the kitchen, you can also use it as a moisturizer for your skin and hair! I call for neutral oil for frying and sautéing throughout the book, and while that could mean any kind of vegetable, grapeseed, or other high-smoke-point oil, refined coconut oil is always a good option. It's colorless and neutral tasting, making it great for frying and baking. Unrefined or "virgin" coconut oil, meanwhile, retains the aroma and flavor of coconut and has a slight yellow tint. You can use this kind of coconut oil for cooking over low to medium heat, or in desserts and dishes where a coconut flavor is desired.

  You'll also see many recipes calling for coconut brown sugar. I particularly love to use coconut brown sugar instead of regular brown sugar in my recipes because it's got this subtle coconut flavor that adds a fun, tropical twist. Plus, it has a lower glycemic index than regular brown sugar, so it won't send your energy levels on a roller-coaster ride like refined sugars can. So if you're watching your sugar intake or just love that coconut vibe like I do, I'd always recommend coconut brown sugar. But hey, there's no sugar-shaming here; regular brown sugar is a reliable option for everyday sweetness.

  Many of my recipes also call for coconut milk. Always choose canned coconut milk, rather than coconut milk in a carton, for best results. Canned coconut milk has a rich, creamy texture and authentic flavor that enhances the depth and character of every dish.

+ MANGOES Mango trees grow in Jamaica as well as Mauritius like apple trees grow in the States – there's a mango tree in many a backyard. Across Jamaica and Mauritius, there are more than fifty varieties of mango, and no two kinds taste the same. Here in the US, you'll find mangoes at your local supermarket or Asian grocery store. But if you can't find them near you, I've included a list of tropical fruit online delivery companies on page 244 so you can get them delivered right to your door. To check whether a mango is ripe, squeeze it gently. A medium-ripe mango will be somewhat firm with some give, but an unripe mango will be very firm to the touch. Some recipes call for green (unripe) mango.

+ TAMARIND This fruit is native to Africa but widely cultivated in tropical regions around the world. It's used in Asian, Middle Eastern, African, and

Latin American cuisine. It has a unique sweet and tangy flavor, often described as a combination of sour cherries and dates. The flavor can vary depending on the ripeness of the fruit, with younger tamarinds being more sour and mature ones having a sweeter taste. It's often used to add a tangy and tart flavor to dishes such as curries; chutneys, sauces, and marinades; and beverages like tamarind lemonade. At your local Asian grocery store, you can find tamarind in different forms, including fresh pods, compressed blocks, concentrate, and paste. The form you choose can depend on your recipe and convenience. Fresh pods are great for extracting pulp, while blocks, concentrates, and pastes offer a more convenient way to incorporate tamarind into dishes. I use tamarind paste for my Tamarind

GLUTEN FREE
USDA
1+1 Two Bags inside
MARQUE
Brown Betty
BRAND
Bedessee
EST. 1977
Guyanese Style
SPECIALTY
Vegan
VEGAN
FISH SAUCE
TROPICAL SUN
JAMAICAN
李錦記
LEE KUM KEE
鮮味生抽
SOY SAUCE
Naturally Brewed
NET 16.9 fl oz (1.05 pt) 500 ml
Nature's Charm
Sweetened Condensed
COCONUT Milk
DAIRY AND SOY FREE
VEGAN
OAT
Whipping
Cream
CHILL POUR WHIP
Condensed
OAT MILK
Caviart
Brad's
Organic
ORGANIC
COCONUT
MILK
Unsweetened
JAMAICAN
Salt Water
CENTO
QUARTERED & MARINATED
NET WT 12 OZ (340g)
THRILLING FOODS
BAKON STRIPS
Thick Sliced
TOUCH OF MAPLE WITH BLACK PEPPERCORN

Vegan Tool Kit

In this cookbook, you'll find a variety of ingredients used as plant-based substitutes for animal protein. Oyster mushrooms make a good stand-in for chicken; tofu can replace just about anything (fish, chicken, and scrambled eggs); banana blossoms also replace fish; and hearts of palm and artichokes are great substitutes for saltfish. Of course, legumes like beans and lentils are a wonderful source of protein as well.

I also occasionally use egg substitutes; plant-based milks, butter, mayo, ice cream, cheese, fish sauce, oyster sauce, and honey; and plant-based meats (e.g., sausages, ground beef, and bacon). I recommend my favorite brands for these products in the recipes when I think it can make a positive impact on your finished dish.

I also share my favorite ingredients for creating depth of flavor and umami, with ingredients like Himalayan black salt for a sulfurous, earthy flavor that tastes like egg; nori and kelp powder, which can add the brininess you'd associate with seafood; and nutritional yeast in a dish that traditionally has cheese. You'll want to check out my killer spice blends, too (see Vegan Island Pantry, page 217).

The following ingredients are my pantry must-haves. In addition to items that are essential for making flavorful vegan meals, you'll also find brands that have founders whom I admire. It's my mission to support as many women as possible, and my cookbook is filled with amazing, innovative plant-based products that women have created. WunderEggs and Yo Egg are shining examples of that dedication and ingenuity.

+ **BRAGG NUTRITIONAL YEAST** This seasoning is a staple for any dish that needs a cheesy boost without the dairy. Whether you're sprinkling it over popcorn, stirring it into creamy sauces, or adding a savory touch to your vegetable dishes, this nutritional yeast is the perfect vegan substitute for Parmesan, plus it is a fantastic source of protein and rich in B vitamins.
+ **CAVI-ART VEGAN SHRIMP** This groundbreaking ingredient by Jens Møller has completely transformed my seafood dishes. This incredible innovation not only captures the texture and flavor of shrimp but does so sustainably and cruelty-free. It is perfect for everything from a shrimp cocktail to a curry, which you can find right here in my cookbook (page 107). The brand also offers plant-based fish roe.

- **CHOBANI OATMILK** Chobani's oat milk is an absolute favorite among plant-based milks, offering versatility and deliciousness in every carton. Their options include an original flavor that's smooth and lovely for everyday use, an extra-creamy variety perfect for rich sauces and decadent mac and cheese, and a zero-sugar version for those watching their sugar intake.
- **HAPPY VIKING** Created by Venus Williams, this is my to go-to daily protein shake.
- **KEYMOSS SEA MOSS** My favorite sea moss gel is made by Keymoss, owned by the amazing husband-and-wife team Jermane and Keke.
- **PLANT-BASED BUTTER** Plant-based butter has indeed come a long way, and there are some fantastic options available that rival traditional butter in flavor and functionality. I personally like both Earth Balance and Violife. Earth Balance offers a rich, creamy texture that's perfect for baking and spreading, while Violife's butter has a wonderful melt and subtle flavor that works beautifully in cooking and as a topping. Whether you're vegan or just looking to reduce dairy in your diet, these plant-based butters are satisfying alternatives that don't compromise on taste or texture.
- **PLANT-BASED FISH SAUCE** I highly recommend the plant-based fish sauce from 24Vegan. This brand is woman owned (by Kimberly Vodang), which I love, and delivers an incredible umami taste that rivals traditional fish sauce and is the most convincing option on the market. Whether you're making a classic noodle dish or just want to enhance your marinades, this all-purpose seasoning is a stellar choice.
- **SOY SAUCE** I usually use Kikkoman for its rich, balanced flavor. But if you're gluten or soy intolerant, there are great alternatives to consider. San-J Tamari Soy Sauce is a gluten-free option that offers a deeper, more robust flavor. Bragg Liquid Aminos is a versatile, soy-based seasoning that's also gluten-free. For a completely soy-free option, try Coconut Secret Coconut Aminos, which has a slightly sweeter taste but works well in any recipe calling for soy sauce.
- **THRILLING FOODS BAKON** If you're searching for a mouthwatering alternative to traditional bacon that aligns with a cruelty-free and environmentally friendly lifestyle, I highly recommend Bakon Strips from Thrilling Foods. Skillfully salt-cured and smoked, these strips deliver all the sizzle, aroma, and texture of classic bacon, but without any harm to animals.
- **VIOLIFE CHEESE** Made from coconut oil and fortified with vitamin B12, Violife melts beautifully and adds a creamy texture that's hard to beat. There is a wide range of flavors and formats, from slices and shreds to blocks and spreads.
- **WUNDEREGGS** Hema Reddy, the trailblazing entrepreneur behind Crafty Counter, has created the world's first vegan hard-boiled egg. Her dedication to quality, sustainability, and crafting delicious vegan eggs like no other is why I wholeheartedly support her and her vision in this cookbook. I had to use her vegan eggs – they're a game-changer!
- **YO EGG** Step into the innovative world of plant-based cuisine with Yo Egg's sunny-side up and poached eggs. These eggs feature a unique runny yolk, offering an authentic experience that's both cholesterol-free and bursting with flavor.

My Essential Kitchen Tools

Welcome to the heart of your kitchen! Let's explore the must-have tools that transform cooking from a chore into a delight. Imagine this space filled with sharp and versatile knives, reliable pots and pans, and shelves stocked with an array of spices, oils, and grains. Whether you're just starting out or you're a seasoned chef, having the right equipment and ingredients readily accessible can dramatically enhance your cooking experience. These are more than just tools and supplies; they are your partners in culinary creativity.

+ **CAST-IRON PAN** The Lodge cast-iron pan is a kitchen hero and my go-to for everything from tempering spices, such as for my Tofu Vindaye (page 87), to searing vegetables like in Jamaican Cabbage and Bacon (page 142). It heats evenly and gives those perfect, crispy edges to vegetables that make plant-based meals so satisfying.
+ **CHEF'S KNIFE** Essential to any kitchen, a good chef's knife is key for precision and efficiency. I use a Nakano 8-inch (20 cm) chef's knife, which is ideal for everything from mincing garlic to slicing vegetables.
+ **CUTTING BOARD** A sturdy, heavy-duty wooden cutting board is the foundation of efficient prep work. Mine has witnessed countless meals come to life, from chopping fresh herbs to dicing hearty vegetables. My preference is a wooden board because it's gentle on your knives, naturally resistant to bacteria, and incredibly durable. Plus, it provides a stable surface that makes every slice, dice, and chop a breeze.
+ **JUICER** An indispensable appliance in my kitchen, the Nama J2 Cold Press Juicer is perfect for extracting fresh, nutrient-rich juices from a variety of fruits and vegetables. Making fresh juices is a daily ritual that energizes me. I've been through a whole lineup of juicers, but the Nama juicer steals the show every time. It's my kitchen MVP, no contest.

- **MASON JARS** Not just for canning, these versatile jars are perfect for storing spices, homemade dressings, or overnight oats. I also use them for serving smoothies and layered salads, adding a touch of rustic charm to the presentation.
- **MORTAR AND PESTLE** This ancient tool releases the full flavor potential of whole spices and herbs. Grinding spices and making pastes is a ritualistic part of my cooking, connecting me to the tactile aspects of food preparation.
- **NONSTICK COOKWARE** The twelve-piece ceramic nonstick cookware set by Drew Barrymore's brand Beautiful is made with a nontoxic ceramic coating that is PTFE, PFOA, and PFOS free.
- **STAINLESS-STEEL STRAINER OR SPIDER FOR FRYING** This tool is perfect for frying up tofu, tempeh, or vegetable fritters. It allows you to carefully remove items from hot oil while leaving any excess oil behind, which is crucial for achieving a crispy texture without the mess.
- **WAFFLE MAKER** The Beautiful rotating Belgian waffle maker by Drew Barrymore is my pick for beauty and function. It is affordable and comes in fun colors. Ideal for more than just breakfast, my waffle maker turns ordinary ingredients like plantains into fun, crispy treats. I love experimenting with different grains and flavors to create sweet and savory vegan waffle batters.
- **WOK** Essential for stir-fries, the wok makes quick work of cooking large amounts of vegetables while preserving their texture and nutrients. If you're looking for the healthiest option, I recommend a carbon-steel wok. They are not only durable and efficient but also free from harmful chemicals and coatings. They heat up quickly and distribute heat evenly, which helps retain the nutrients in your ingredients. Look for a flat-bottomed carbon-steel wok for stability on modern stovetops. With proper care and seasoning, this wok will become a versatile tool in your kitchen.

YOU MUST
PAY FIRST
BEFORE PICKING
UP YOUR FISH
THANK YOU
MANAGEMENT
TURBANA

12 OZ.
CHIEF
Green Seasoning
JFK

BREAKFAST

Breakfast is serious business in a Jamaican household. It's never just a bowl of cereal, but a heavy, solid meal that will give you the strength and vitality you need to get through your entire day.

During my childhood, Sundays were epic breakfast days in our family—that's when my dad would pull out all the stops, putting music on, frying dumplings to pair with ackee, and sipping on carrot juice. On most days, I usually prefer a lighter breakfast; I'll go for a smoothie, açaí bowl, or a juice. But on Sundays, I still practice my family's tradition of going all out.

In this section, I've included a variety of breakfast ideas, from quick and easy to hearty and comforting, to prepare you for whatever your day holds.

Jamaican "No Saltfish" Fritters

SERVES 4

Let's dive in with my vegan saltfish fritters—a delicious dish that brings the vibrant flavors of Jamaica to your table with NO saltfish! Imagine a kitchen filled with the aroma of spices and the sizzling sounds of a frying pan—that's the kind of magic we're stirring up!

If you're new to Jamaican cuisine, these fritters are a must-try. They offer a unique blend of salty, savory, and slightly spicy flavors, all encapsulated in a crispy, golden-brown exterior. A perfect introduction to the island's love for richly seasoned and hearty foods, they're a staple in Jamaican households. Traditionally popular at breakfast, they also make for an excellent appetizer or side dish, pairing wonderfully with a variety of sauces for dipping.

The key ingredient in the traditional fritters, saltfish, or dried fish, is a white fish (usually cod) that has been preserved by salt-curing. A feature of Caribbean cuisine since the Europeans introduced it centuries ago, saltfish is still a favorite ingredient in Jamaica today because of its firm, slightly chewy texture, and also because it is more flavorful than fresh fish from the salting.

But have no fear: I discovered a plant-based solution that mimics the texture and briny taste. In fact, for those not a fan of fishy flavors, my recipe might even be better than the original. In place of the usual salted cod, we'll be marinating artichokes, allowing them to soak up a blend of incredible Caribbean spices.

In this cookbook, you'll see both artichoke and hearts of palm standing in for fish. I prefer using artichokes in this recipe because their flaky texture is delightful when deep-fried. I use hearts of palm when I want more-solid pieces that will hold up in stir-fries. For a "no fish" recipe with hearts of palm, check out my Ackee and "No Saltfish" (page 42).

1 (14-ounce/400 g) can artichoke hearts in brine

¼ cup (15 g) finely chopped scallions

½ cup (90 g) chopped tomato

1 medium white onion, finely chopped

¼ cup (35 g) diced green bell pepper

¼ cup (35 g) diced red bell pepper

1 Scotch bonnet pepper, seeded and finely chopped (see Notes, page 38)

½ teaspoon baking powder

1½ cups (190 g) all-purpose flour

½ teaspoon ground black pepper

1 teaspoon paprika

1 teaspoon Old Bay seasoning

Drain the artichoke hearts and shred them into strips with your fingers, breaking each quarter of an artichoke heart into about 4 pieces.

In a large mixing bowl, add the shredded artichokes, scallions, tomato, onion, bell peppers, thyme, all-purpose seasoning, and Scotch bonnet pepper. Sprinkle the baking powder over the vegetables and toss to combine.

Pour 1 cup (240 ml) water into the bowl.

Gradually add the flour to the bowl, mixing continuously. The mix should be slightly sloppy, not too thick or runny, to allow

for easy spooning into the pan. Adjust the consistency by adding a little more water or flour if necessary.

Add the black pepper, paprika, and Old Bay seasoning, then mix thoroughly to ensure the spices are evenly distributed.

In a large frying pan, heat 1 inch (2.5 cm) of oil over high heat. Test the oil temperature by dropping a small amount of batter into the oil; it should sizzle instantly when hot enough. Using a teaspoon, scoop up a portion of the batter and carefully drop it into the hot oil, forming each fritter to be about the size of a flattened golf ball (see Notes). Do not overcrowd the pan – there should space between each fritter while cooking so that you can flip them easily.

Reduce the heat to medium. This helps to cook the fritters through without burning the exterior. Fry the fritters, flipping once, until they are golden brown on each side, 3 to 4 minutes per side, depending on their size.

Once cooked, transfer the fritters to a plate lined with paper towels to drain. Repeat with the remaining batter.

Serve the fritters hot accompanied by Scotch bonnet mango hot sauce.

Green Banana Porridge

SERVES 4 TO 6

I invite you to step into my grandma Bernice's kitchen on a cozy Sunday morning, where this rich, creamy porridge was usually bubbling on the stove, ready to sustain us through even the longest church services.

This hearty and nutritious dish offers a unique, subtly sweet flavor with an earthy undertone, thanks to the green bananas, which are less sweet and starchier than their ripe counterparts. When cooked down, the bananas develop a creamy texture that is both satisfying and comforting.

Green bananas are rich in resistant starch, which acts like fiber, aiding in digestion and helping to regulate blood sugar levels. They are also a good source of vitamins, particularly vitamins C and B6, and minerals like potassium, which supports heart health and blood pressure regulation. Overall, this porridge provides a balanced mix of carbohydrates, vitamins, and minerals, making it a wholesome, delicious breakfast.

- 3 green (unripe) bananas, peeled and finely grated
- 1 cup (240 ml) oat milk
- 1 (13½-ounce/400 ml) can unsweetened coconut milk
- ¼ teaspoon ground nutmeg, plus more for garnish
- 1 teaspoon vanilla extract
- ⅛ teaspoon Himalayan pink salt
- About ⅓ cup (79 ml) sweetened condensed coconut milk, such as Nature's Charm
- ¼ teaspoon ground cinnamon or 2 cinnamon sticks (optional)
- Coconut brown sugar, for garnish
- Coconut flakes, for garnish

In a medium saucepan, bring 3 cups (720 ml) water to a boil over high heat. Add the bananas, oat milk, coconut milk, nutmeg, vanilla extract, and pink salt and stir until fully combined.

Cook uncovered over medium heat for 30 minutes, stirring occasionally to prevent sticking (see Note).

Stir in the condensed coconut milk a little at a time, tasting as you go, adding more or less depending on how sweet you like it. Add the cinnamon, if using, and continue cooking for 5 to 10 minutes, until the porridge reaches your desired consistency.

Remove the cinnamon sticks, if necessary, and serve the porridge immediately, sprinkling a bit of nutmeg and coconut brown sugar on top.

NOTE

SPLASH ZONE SAFETY: When cooking this porridge, the mixture can pop or splatter as it thickens and bubbles, similar to making oatmeal. To avoid any mishaps, it's wise to stir the porridge regularly and keep the heat at a moderate level. Using a deep pot can also help minimize splattering, and you can use a splatter guard as an extra precaution.

Ackee and "No Saltfish"

SERVES 4 TO 6

As a child, waking up to the comforting aromas of salted cod and ackee was a regular delight. Now, my vegan version of Jamaica's national dish and favorite breakfast takes me back to those carefree days, filled with warmth and endless possibilities. Each bite is a reminder of home, where the food was hearty and the laughter loud, and where every day held new adventures.

Ackee is a savory fruit native to West Africa that came to Jamaica along with enslaved Africans. Outside of Jamaica, ackee isn't sold fresh but is easy to find canned even in mainstream supermarkets and, of course, online. Ackee's soft texture and subtle nutty flavor complement the flavors of other ingredients, tempering the saltiness and firm, dry texture of saltfish and absorbing the aromatic qualities of peppers and onions.

My recipe captures the essence of this beloved Jamaican breakfast and the unique, heartwarming flavors of the island. Using hearts of palm as a substitute for the fish maintains the traditional texture and richness while crumbled nori and kelp powder bring a briny, fishlike taste.

With this dish, I invite you to savor a piece of Jamaican culture, embrace a meal that diverges from the typical Western breakfast, and discover flavors that might be entirely new to you. It's more than breakfast—it's a culinary adventure and a journey home.

I love pairing this with Jamaican Fried Dumplings, as you can see on page 44, or my Plantain Breakfast Waffle (page 47) for a complete meal. To make it a real feast, add some sliced avocado, Fried Plantains (page 150), and Callaloo Sauté (page 141).

FOR THE "NO SALTFISH":

- 1 (14-ounce/397 g) can hearts of palm, drained
- 1 tablespoon salt
- 4 snack sheets nori (such as Gimme Organic or One Organic), crumbled
- 2 teaspoons kelp powder

FOR COOKING AND SERVING:

- Refined coconut oil or neutral oil, for frying
- 2 tablespoons store-bought fish seasoning mix, such as Mimi's
- Vegan fish sauce, such as 24Vegan (optional)
- Salt and ground black pepper
- 3 cloves garlic, finely diced
- 1 (1-inch/2.5 cm) piece fresh ginger, peeled and finely minced
- 2 Roma tomatoes, roughly chopped
- 1 green bell pepper, roughly chopped
- ½ red onion, roughly chopped
- 3 scallions, sliced
- ¼ Scotch bonnet pepper or more for your preferred heat, finely diced (optional)
- 3 or 4 sprigs thyme
- ¼ cup (60 ml) canned unsweetened coconut milk
- ¼ cup (60 ml) tomato paste
- 1 (19-ounce/540 g) can ackee, drained, liquid and ackee saved separately

TO PREPARE THE "NO SALTFISH":

The day before serving, cut the hearts of palm in half lengthwise, then diagonally, and shred them slightly to achieve a saltfish look.

To a Mason jar, add the shredded hearts of palm, 1 cup (240 ml) water, the salt, crumbled nori, and kelp powder. Pop the lid on the jar and set aside at room temperature overnight.

TO COOK THE "NO SALTFISH" AND ACKEE:

Drain the hearts of palm and pat dry. Heat 1 tablespoon coconut oil in a large skillet over high heat. Transfer the hearts of palm to the skillet, season with the fish seasoning, vegan fish sauce, if using, and black pepper, and fry until brown and crisp. Remove the hearts of palm to a paper towel–lined plate and set aside.

In the same skillet, heat 1 tablespoon oil over medium heat. Add the garlic, ginger, tomatoes, bell pepper, red onion, scallions, and Scotch bonnet, if using. Cook until the red onion is soft and translucent, 5 to 8 minutes. Add the thyme, coconut milk, tomato paste, and the liquid from the ackee can. Cover and simmer for 15 minutes.

Stir in the hearts of palm, then cover the mixture with a layer of ackee. DO NOT STIR; let the ackee sit on top. Season with salt and black pepper to taste.

Cover the skillet and let it warm through on low heat for an additional 15 minutes, until the ackee is heated through. Remove the sprigs of thyme and serve.

Jamaican Fried Dumplings

MAKES 6 DUMPLINGS

Jamaican fried dumplings, often called "johnnycakes," play a significant role in Jamaican cuisine and culture. These fried breads are a staple in Jamaican breakfasts and are also enjoyed throughout the day as a snack or side dish. They are made from a simple dough of flour, salt, and baking powder that is then fried until golden brown and crispy on the outside and soft and fluffy on the inside.

In Jamaica, fried dumplings are a symbol of comfort, home, and togetherness. They are often served alongside traditional Jamaican dishes like ackee and saltfish (see page 42) and greens like the Callaloo Sauté (page 141), as shown here.

Fried dumplings represent the resourcefulness of Jamaican cooks, who have historically created delicious and filling dishes using simple and readily available ingredients. They are also a symbol of hospitality, as sharing food, especially a hearty and satisfying dish like fried dumplings, is a common way of welcoming guests in Jamaican culture.

1 cup (125 g) all-purpose flour, sifted

1½ teaspoons baking powder

Pinch of salt

½ tablespoon unsalted plant-based butter, such as Earth Balance, at room temperature

Neutral oil, for frying

In a medium bowl, whisk together the flour, baking powder, and salt.

Add the butter to the dry ingredients. Use a fork to work the butter into the flour mixture until it forms a sandy, crumb-like texture.

Gradually pour ⅓ cup (80 ml) water into the flour mixture while mixing with your hands to form a dough. The dough should be soft and pliable, like a bread dough – smooth and elastic, but not too sticky. If it is too sticky, you can add a little flour. Leave the dough in the bowl and cover the bowl with plastic wrap. Allow it to rise at room temperature for about 1 hour.

After the dough has risen, divide the dough into 6 pieces. Form each piece into a round dumpling shape; I usually make them 2 to 3 inches (5 to 7.5 cm) in diameter and ½ inch (12 mm) thick.

Pour oil into a large nonstick pan to a depth of ¾ inch (2 cm). Heat the oil over low to medium heat until it reaches around 350°F (175°C) when measured with a deep-fry thermometer.

Working in batches of 3 at a time, carefully place the formed dumplings into the pan and fry for 6 to 8 minutes per side, gently flipping the dumplings to ensure even cooking, until golden brown and cooked through. Remove them from the oil and place on a paper towel to absorb the excess oil.

Serve immediately while hot.

Matouk's
CALYPSO
SAUCE

Plantain Breakfast Waffle

MAKES 1 WAFFLE

My waffle maker is my best friend—and I don't just stop at regular waffles. I've tossed into it everything from casava and green bananas to sweet potatoes. But my all-time favorite? Plantain waffles. Savory with crunchy, caramelized edges, these are delicious when drizzled with a slightly sweet, slightly tart passion fruit vinaigrette and paired with cool, creamy avocado and a perfectly ripe tomato. Once you make this, you'll never go back to regular waffles. Get ready for a breakfast remix like no other!

And this is even better with my Ackee and "No Saltfish" (page 42). The combination of sweet, crispy plantains with creamy ackee is heavenly. The ackee melts in your mouth, adding a smooth, buttery contrast. With its vibrant flavors and a delightful play of textures, this duo is sure to impress any breakfast or brunch crowd.

FOR THE WAFFLE:

2 ripe plantains

Refined coconut oil or neutral oil, for brushing the waffle maker

½ avocado, sliced

½ cup (270 g) Ackee and "No Saltfish" (page 42)

1 Scotch bonnet pepper, thinly sliced

Chopped scallions

Chopped tomato

FOR THE PASSION FRUIT VINAIGRETTE:

½ cup (120 ml) passion fruit juice

2 tablespoons olive oil

2 tablespoons apple cider vinegar

1 tablespoon agave

Salt and ground black pepper

Pinch of red pepper flakes (optional)

EQUIPMENT:

Steamer basket

Waffle maker

TO MAKE THE WAFFLE:

Peel the plantains and cut them crosswise into 3 pieces each. Check to ensure that these pieces can be arranged to cover the surface area of the waffle maker, leaving a little space around the outer edge so they won't spill out when pressed later. Place the plantains in a steamer basket in a single layer.

Prepare a pot for steaming by filling it with just enough water to not touch the bottom of your steamer basket. Bring the water to a simmer over medium heat.

Place the steamer basket with the plantains into the pot and cover. Steam the plantains for 15 minutes, or until they are tender and can be easily pierced with a fork.

Preheat the waffle maker following the manufacturer's instructions. Brush the waffle maker with oil to prevent sticking.

Place the steamed plantains on the waffle maker and gently close the waffle maker, ensuring they are evenly spaced and cover the entire surface to form a full waffle. Cook until the plantains turn golden brown, 5 to 6 minutes.

MEANWHILE, MAKE THE PASSION FRUIT VINAIGRETTE:

In a bowl, whisk together the passion fruit juice, olive oil, vinegar, agave, salt, black pepper, and red pepper flakes, if using.

Top the waffle with the avocado, ackee and "no saltfish," if using, Scotch bonnet, if you want that extra kick of spice, scallion, and tomato. Drizzle with the passion fruit dressing and serve immediately.

Breakfast Cereal Sea Moss Shake

SERVES 2

If you grew up Jamaican like me, you know sea moss isn't just something you find in health food stores—it's a vital part of our culinary heritage. Preparing sea moss is an art: we dry it under the tropical sun, then blend it into a rich, creamy gel.

Grown in Jamaica's pristine waters, sea moss is a powerhouse of essential nutrients. Packed with iodine, calcium, potassium, and magnesium, it supports the immune system, aids digestion, and promotes optimal energy levels. Whether we're adding it to smoothies for a nutritious kick, using it to thicken up a hearty stew, or even spreading it on as a skin-soothing face mask, sea moss is our go-to superfood.

While the traditional process of preparing sea moss is deeply rooted in our culture, it's wonderful to see how accessible it has become. Now you can find sea moss gel ready-made in many stores, allowing you to enjoy its benefits without the need for elaborate preparation. The convenience of premade sea moss gel makes it easier than ever to embrace this nutrient-rich treasure that has been a part of Jamaican heritage for generations.

Sea moss has a mild, slightly briny taste with a hint of seaweed's freshness. Its flavor can vary but is generally neutral, making it versatile for use in various dishes without overpowering other flavors. When turned into gel, as shown in the bowl on the opposite page, its taste becomes even milder, making it a popular addition to smoothies, soups, and desserts for its nutritional benefits alone.

Embrace the natural benefits of sea moss with this quick and easy shake that is nutty and irresistibly creamy from the bananas.

- 2 cups (480 ml) almond milk
- 1 cup (150 g) your favorite granola
- 2 bananas, peeled
- 2 tablespoons sunflower seed butter
- 1 tablespoon flax seeds
- ¼ cup (60 ml) flavorless, organic sea moss gel, such as Keymoss Sea Moss
- 1 cup (220 g) ice cubes

To a blender, add the almond milk, granola, bananas, sunflower seed butter, flax seeds, sea moss gel, and ice and blend until smooth.

Pour the shake into two glasses and serve immediately.

Cacao, Sea Moss, and Maca Smoothie Bowl

SERVES 1

This morning bowl will rock your taste buds, but it's also full of nourishing ingredients to give your body the kick start it needs!

First up, cacao—which brings way more to the table than just chocolatey bliss. This stuff is a superhero in disguise, packed with antioxidants that swoop in and shield your cells from the chaos of daily life. Plus, it's like a secret mood elevator, triggering happy hormones and setting a positive vibe for the day.

Next, meet maca—the natural energizer. This powder brings a gentle boost without the crazy jitters. It's like Mother Nature's way of saying, "Wake up and slay the day!" Maca has a unique taste that can be described as earthy, nutty, and slightly sweet with a hint of butterscotch or caramel undertones. Its flavor profile is often compared to that of a cross between a potato and a nut, but with a subtle sweetness.

Put cacao and maca together, and you've got a dynamic duo. They're like the Bonnie and Clyde of your morning routine, taking on oxidative stress, supporting your heart, and helping your brain focus.

But it's the toppings that take center stage in this smoothie bowl. A lavish drizzle of creamy peanut butter adds a decadent touch and a velvety texture that pairs perfectly with the smoothie's richness. Nutrient-rich chia seeds bring a satisfying crunch and a burst of health benefits with every bite. And bananas offer a natural sweetness and freshness that complements the smoothie's chocolate and earthy notes.

FOR THE SMOOTHIE:

- 2 frozen peeled bananas
- 2 tablespoons raw cacao powder
- 2 tablespoons flavorless, organic sea moss gel, such as Keymoss Sea Moss
- 1½ tablespoons raw maca powder
- 1 cup (240 ml) unsweetened oat milk
- ⅛ teaspoon ground cinnamon

FOR THE TOPPINGS (OPTIONAL):

- Peanut butter
- Chia seeds
- Sliced bananas
- Dried coconut
- Cacao nibs

To a blender, add the bananas, cacao powder, sea moss gel, maca powder, oat milk, and cinnamon and blend until smooth.

Pour into a bowl, add as many toppings as you wish, and serve immediately.

Tropical Charcoal Detox Smoothie Bowl

SERVES 1

My daughter and I aren't usually big eaters on weekday mornings, but this smoothie bowl is always a winner. It's a delightful and refreshing way to embrace the day.

Activated charcoal stars in this bowl, bringing more than just a dramatic color. Known for its detoxifying properties, activated charcoal helps cleanse your body and promotes a healthy gut. As you enjoy this laid-back treat, relish not only the flavors but the health benefits that come with every spoonful.

You can get creative with your toppings, but I like to sprinkle some chia seeds for extra texture and fiber; add a generous handful of pumpkin seeds or nuts for a delightful crunch and a boost of healthy fats; and then complete the masterpiece with an array of fruits, like blueberries and coconut, to elevate both the flavor and aesthetics.

FOR THE SMOOTHIE:

1 frozen peeled banana

¼ cup (40 g) frozen blueberries

¼ cup (60 g) frozen pineapple

2 teaspoons activated charcoal powder

1 teaspoon mushroom powder

½ cup (120 ml) coconut water

Handful of spinach

FOR THE TOPPINGS (OPTIONAL):

Chia seeds

Nuts

Berries and/or fruit, chopped, such as mango, banana, and coconut

To a blender, add the banana, blueberries, pineapple, charcoal powder, mushroom powder, coconut water, and spinach. Blend until smooth, ensuring a luscious, creamy consistency.

Pour the smoothie into a bowl and top with your favorite seeds, nuts, and fruits, as desired, and serve immediately.

USA
503 BROADWAY - SOHO

Super Fluffy "Bacon" Pancakes

SERVES 2

In my late twenties, I embarked on an unforgettable journey, touring Japan with the band Incognito. Among the many highlights of this experience were the hotel breakfasts—they were a food lover's dream! Japanese pancakes always stole the show; I swear they're the best in the world!

Today, I've taken it upon myself to re-create these fluffy pancakes in my own kitchen. White vinegar makes them much fluffier than American pancakes, and I've added an unexpected twist: bacon. Yes, despite my vegan lifestyle, the allure of bacon has lingered. Thanks to Thrilling Foods and their plant-based sorcery, I've crafted fluffy vegan pancakes that envelop pieces of savory bacon—an unexpected delight for breakfast enthusiasts everywhere.

But the magic doesn't stop there! I love infusing my dishes with a tropical island twist. Enter a blend of nutmeg, cinnamon, and vanilla paired with banana. This is my fusion of a Jamaican banana fritter and a fluffy pancake, creating a symphony of flavors that's simply irresistible.

5 strips plant-based bacon strips, such as Thrilling Foods

2 cups (250 g) all-purpose flour

2 tablespoons confectioners' sugar

3 teaspoons baking powder

1 teaspoon baking soda

1 teaspoon ground cinnamon

1 teaspoon ground nutmeg

4 tablespoons neutral oil, plus more for frying

2 tablespoons distilled white vinegar

1½ cups (345 ml) unsweetened plant-based milk (add a splash more if the batter is too thick, as some plant-based milks are thicker than others)

2 teaspoons vanilla extract

1 banana, smashed

Unsalted plant-based butter, such as Earth Balance, for serving

Maple syrup, for serving

Preheat the oven to 200°F (90°C).

Slice your bacon into pieces. The bacon pieces will be placed at the center of each pancake, so you can adjust the size of your slices based on your preferred pancake size, as needed. I like to make my pancakes about 4 inches (10 cm) in diameter. So I usually cut each strip into 4 pieces. If there are leftovers, you can always serve them alongside the pancakes or save them for a snack.

In a medium pan over medium heat, fry the bacon pieces until crispy. Set aside.

In a medium bowl, combine the flour, confectioners' sugar, baking powder, baking soda, cinnamon, and nutmeg. Add the oil and vinegar, then combine.

Pour in the milk, vanilla extract, and smashed banana and stir until just combined, being careful not to overmix.

In a medium pan, heat the oil over medium-low heat.

Place one bacon square in the pan and pour ⅓ cup (40 g) pancake mix over the bacon.

Continued

Super Fluffy "Bacon" Pancakes

CONTINUED

Add another piece of bacon on top of the pancake. Cover the pan and cook the pancake until its edges are golden brown. Flip the pancake and continue cooking, uncovered, until the second side is golden brown.

Transfer the pancake to a baking sheet and place in the oven to keep warm. Repeat with the remaining bacon and pancake batter.

Serve the pancakes immediately with butter and a drizzle of maple syrup.

NOTE

While you don't need to use the tool I'm holding in the photo on the opposite page—it's actually meant for icing cakes—I like to use it to make my pancakes a perfect circle. But don't worry, it's not necessary for the recipe. Your pancakes will turn out just as delicious without it!

Tropical Pancakes with Pan-Grilled Pineapple

SERVES 2

Get ready for a tropical breakfast delight that showcases my vegan take on a classic American pancake, paired with the vibrant flavor of sun-soaked pineapple! This fusion of sweet and tangy goodness is sure to brighten your mornings. There's something about grilled, caramelized pineapple that adds an irresistible depth of flavor and sweetness to each bite.

FOR THE PAN-GRILLED PINEAPPLE:

- 1 teaspoon ground cinnamon
- 1 teaspoon ground nutmeg
- 2 teaspoons vanilla extract
- 2 tablespoons coconut brown sugar
- 2 tablespoons salted plant-based butter, such as Earth Balance, melted
- 1 pineapple, peeled and cut into ½-inch-thick (12 mm) slices

FOR THE PANCAKES:

- 1 cup (125 g) all-purpose flour
- 2 tablespoons coconut brown sugar
- 1 teaspoon ground cinnamon
- 1 teaspoon baking powder
- ½ teaspoon baking soda
- ½ cup (45 g) unsweetened coconut flakes
- 3 tablespoons neutral oil, plus more for frying
- 1 tablespoon distilled white vinegar
- 1½ cups (360 ml) canned unsweetened coconut milk

FOR THE TOPPINGS (OPTIONAL):

- Unsweetened coconut flakes
- Fresh mint leaves

TO GRILL THE PINEAPPLE:

In a small bowl, combine the cinnamon, nutmeg, vanilla extract, brown sugar, and melted butter. Stir until the ingredients form a smooth mixture.

Heat a grill pan over medium-high heat and place the pineapple slices directly onto the hot pan. Brush the melted butter mixture over the pineapple, flipping each slice to coat both sides.

Grill the pineapple slices for approximately 2 minutes on each side, or until grill marks appear and the pineapple caramelizes slightly. This step adds smokiness and enhances the natural sweetness of the fruit.

Once pan-grilled to perfection, remove the pineapple slices from the heat and set aside to cool.

TO MAKE THE PANCAKES:

In a medium bowl, combine the flour, brown sugar, cinnamon, baking powder, baking soda, and coconut flakes.

Add the oil and vinegar to the bowl and mix to combine. Pour in the coconut milk and stir until just combined, being careful not to overmix.

In a pan, heat 1 tablespoon oil over medium-low heat. Ladle ¼ cup (60 ml) of batter into the pan and cook the pancakes, covered, until the edges are golden brown and you see bubbles forming in the middle of the pancake. Flip the pancake and continue cooking, uncovered, until the second side is golden brown. Repeat with the remaining batter, adding oil to the pan as needed between batches.

Top the pancakes with the grilled pineapple. Serve the pancakes with a sprinkle of coconut flakes and fresh mint leaves.

Mango Chile Lassi

SERVES 2

In Mauritius, lassi is a beloved beverage that reflects the island's Indian heritage. It's a refreshing and slightly sweet drink typically made with yogurt, water, and sugar, often incorporating other local ingredients, such as tropical fruits like mango, pineapple, or lychee, and accented by cardamom, red saffron, chiles, or a hint of rose water. Especially enjoyed as a cooling drink during warm days or as a refreshing accompaniment to spicy Mauritian dishes, lassis have a creamy texture; the blend of sweet and tangy flavors makes it a popular choice among locals and visitors alike.

Luckily, you don't need to make the journey to experience this delight. I've perfected a vegan version of the recipe, bringing the essence of Mauritius and its incredible mango lassi straight to your kitchen.

FOR THE LASSI:

- 1 cup (240 ml) canned mango pulp
- 1 cup (240 ml) plain almond milk yogurt, or any dairy-free or vegan yogurt
- ½ cup (120 ml) unsweetened plant-based milk
- 1 fresh red chile pepper (or ½ teaspoon chili powder)
- ¼ teaspoon ground cardamom
- 1 tablespoon ground turmeric
- 1 Medjool date, such as Natural Delights
- 1 cup (220 g) ice cubes

FOR THE TOPPINGS (OPTIONAL):

- Caradmom pods
- Crushed pistachios

To a blender, add the mango, yogurt, milk, chile pepper, cardamom, turmeric, date, and ice and blend until smooth.

Transfer the mixture to two glasses, add your preferred toppings, and serve immediately.

Jamaican Avocado Toast with Fried Plantains

SERVES 1

Indulge in a taste of Jamaican paradise with my special twist on the classic avocado toast. This hearty and filling breakfast is a celebration of flavors and textures, featuring the beloved Jamaican hard dough bread as its sturdy foundation. Each slice is generously adorned with creamy avocado (which we affectionately call "pear" in Jamaica), crowned with caramelized fried plantains, and finished with a tantalizing drizzle of homemade mango hot sauce. It truly hits different!

2 slices hard dough bread, toasted (see Note)

1 Fried Plantain (page 150), made with plant-based hot honey, sliced

1 avocado, sliced

1 lime wedge

Salt and ground black pepper

Scotch Bonnet Mango Hot Sauce (optional; page 225)

Arrange the fried plantain on the toasted bread, then place the avocado on top of the plantain. Squeeze a lime wedge over the toast, season with salt and pepper to taste, and, if using, drizzle with hot sauce.

NOTE

HARD DOUGH BREAD: This is a popular type of bread in the Caribbean, especially in Jamaica. It's less hydrated than softer breads and known for its dense, chewy texture. Hard dough bread is used for a variety of dishes, particularly hearty sandwiches. Some hard dough breads have milk in them, so be sure to check the ingredients. You can find it in Caribbean markets, or in a pinch, you can always try this tropical approach to avocado toast on your favorite sourdough.

Coconut Brown Sugar Rice Pudding

SERVES 4

This flavorful take on rice pudding is a treat my mum used to whip up for breakfast with the leftover brown rice that sat in the fridge, waiting to be transformed.

Blending cooked brown rice with creamy oat milk, aromatic spices, and the sweetness of coconut brown sugar creates a mosaic of flavors that warms your body and soul, taking you back to simpler times, when every spoonful could bring comfort and joy. While the bowls shown here are simply topped with coconut brown sugar and coconut flakes, I have also been known to spice up this nostalgic dessert with even more flavor and some crunch by adding a combination of different toppings (see Note).

2 cups (480 ml) unsweetened oat milk

2 cups (400 g) cooked brown rice

2 green cardamom pods, slightly crushed

½ teaspoon unsalted plant-based butter, such as Earth Balance

⅛ teaspoon salt

2 tablespoons coconut brown sugar, plus more for serving

1 teaspoon cornstarch

½ teaspoon vanilla extract

Ground cinnamon

Ground nutmeg

Unsweetened coconut flakes

In a heavy-bottomed medium pot or saucepan over medium heat, bring the oat milk to a gentle simmer.

Add the brown rice, cardamom pods, butter, and salt. Stir the mixture until the butter melts.

In a small bowl, combine the brown sugar, cornstarch, and vanilla extract. Add this mixture to the rice and oat milk mixture, stirring continuously.

Continue to simmer the mixture over medium heat, stirring constantly, until its consistency is similar to loose oatmeal, about 5 minutes.

Remove the cardamom pods and ladle the pudding into serving bowls. Enjoy the pudding right away while warm, or refrigerate until cold. You can store the pudding covered in the fridge for up to 3 days.

Dust with a sprinkle of cinnamon, nutmeg, coconut brown sugar, coconut flakes, or any of your favorite toppings (see Note) before serving.

NOTE

These are my favorite toppings:

PISTACHIO ROSE: For a beautiful bowl and an exotic flavor pairing, sprinkle ground pistachios and edible dried rose petals on your rice pudding.

CINNAMON WALNUT: To amp up the comforting flavors of this dish, prepare a mixture of chopped walnuts, brown sugar, and cinnamon to top your pudding.

COCONUT MANGO: For a tropical twist, top each bowl with sliced mango, shredded coconut, and a drizzle of agave.

Feel free to get creative and mix and match these toppings based on your preferences.

Tropical Plantain and "Egg" Breakfast Sandwiches

MAKES 2 SANDWICHES

On Sunday mornings, my dad would take center stage in the kitchen, setting the tone with the soulful tunes of Beres Hammond. The gentle hum of familiar melodies blended harmoniously with the clatter of pans and the sizzle of plantains. As the music enveloped us, the kitchen would transform into a sanctuary of comfort and connection.

In Dad's honor, I make a point of re-creating the same magic and warmth in my home on Sundays. It's an homage to his legacy that extends beyond the food on the table.

Likewise, this breakfast sandwich is greater than the sum of its parts, showing the cultural intersection of Jamaican and British influences. I encourage you to make it against a backdrop of Beres Hammond's timeless melodies.

I like to pair these sandwiches with a generous serving of Haricots Rouges (Spiced Red Kidney Beans; see page 146).

Fried Plantains (page 150)

Knob of unsalted plant-based butter, such as Earth Balance, plus more for the toast

1 (14-ounce/397 g) block tofu of your preferred style (see Note)

2 tablespoons Eggy Seasoning Mix (page 232)

Salt and ground black pepper (optional)

Nutritional yeast (optional)

Ground turmeric (optional)

4 slices hard dough bread, toasted (see Note, page 62)

Scotch Bonnet Mango Hot Sauce (optional; page 225)

Preheat the oven to 200°F (90°C).

Make the fried plantains as directed on page 150. When the fried plantains are cool enough to handle, slice them into bite-size pieces. Transfer the slices to a baking sheet and keep them warm in the oven.

Place the same pan in which you fried the plantains over medium heat, add the butter, and heat until sizzling. Crumble the tofu into the pan.

Sprinkle in the eggy seasoning mix. Stir to evenly distribute the spices. Cook the tofu over medium heat for 5 to 7 minutes, stirring occasionally, until slightly browned. As the tofu cooks, feel free to taste and adjust the seasoning. You might want to add a little more salt, pepper, nutritional yeast, or turmeric.

Once the tofu is as browned as you want it, assemble the sandwiches: Butter the toasted hard dough bread. Take 2 slices of toast and arrange 2 or 3 slices of the fried plantain on each piece of toast. Pile the scrambled eggs on top of the plantains. And if you like, drizzle the sandwiches with a little hot sauce. Then, top each sandwich with another piece of toast.

NOTE

MAINS

Welcome to the heart of my journey, where a single dish is not just a solitary star on the plate but a symphony of flavors, textures, and cultures.

In this book, a main course isn't a singular entity; it's a meeting of influences and roots that have shaped our identity. In each of the recipes in this section, four or five components come together in harmony.

From the vibrant and bold spices reminiscent of Africa to the intricate flavors borrowed from India, the rich heritage of China, and the unique Creole spices that tie it all together—each element on the plate tells a story.

Every bite celebrates a diverse tapestry of tastes that has evolved through generations. Whether it's the aromatic curry from the streets of Jamaica or the savory rougaille from the melting pot of Mauritius, these main dishes create a cultural mosaic on your plate.

Join me as we explore the beauty of a main course that transcends borders, and get ready to savor each one not only as a dish, but as an experience.

Rougaille Dizef (Eggs in Tomato Sauce)

SERVES 4

Rougaille is a cornerstone of Mauritian cuisine, a classic tomato-based Creole sauce. Despite its humble appearance, rougaille is a complex blend of herbs, spices, and the warmth of island cooking, lending depth and character to a variety of dishes.

In my home, a particular favorite that graces our table at least once a week is this sumptuous rougaille dizef, traditionally made with eggs but reimagined here to embrace the vegan lifestyle without sacrificing the soul of Mauritian cooking.

This version of rougaille, perfect for brunch or a quick supper, incorporates a revolutionary product that has changed the way I approach vegan cooking: WunderEggs. Created with care by my friends at Crafty Counter, a woman- and BIPOC-owned business, WunderEggs are a marvel of culinary innovation, perfectly capturing the essence and texture of hard-boiled eggs without any animal products. It's an example of how traditional dishes can evolve to meet modern dietary choices while still honoring cultural heritage.

6 cups (1.4 L) Rougaille Sauce (page 133)

4 WunderEggs vegan hard-boiled eggs, halved

Chopped fresh cilantro, for garnish

Sliced green chiles, for garnish

Ground black pepper

Steamed white basmati rice, for serving

In a large pan over medium heat, heat the rougaille sauce until it is simmering.

Place the egg halves into the sauce. Cover the pan and let the eggs warm for 5 minutes, until heated through.

Garnish with cilantro, chiles, and a sprinkle of black pepper. Serve immediately with hot, steamy rice.

Bol Renversé (Magic Bowl)

SERVES 1

Found on Chinese restaurant menus and in cafés dotted across the island of Mauritius, the Creole Bol Renversé is a testament to the vibrant melting pot of cultures on the island. It was a beloved meal of my mother's; I remember her eating it while she enjoyed her favorite sitcom, crunching on a super-hot green chile.

This recipe is all about the layers, and the magic is in Bol Renversé's presentation. We layer all the components in a bowl (glass if available, so the layers can be seen), starting with a vibrant stir-fry of any vegetables you have on hand—snap peas, broccoli, and carrots are my personal favorites—all brought together with a rich, savory sauce; then we blanket the veggies with a layer of fluffy rice. We cover the bowl with a plate, flip it over, and reveal an upside-down masterpiece! Simply top it with a vegan fried egg, and you have a dish that's as delightful to unveil as it is to eat.

This marvel of culinary creativity beautifully encapsulates how my family has embraced plant-based eating without skimping on tradition or taste. Through this simple yet profound dish, let's celebrate the beauty of plant-based food together, one upside-down bowl at a time.

I love to pair this dish with chutneys (pages 220, 222–224)—the more the merrier!

5 dried shiitake mushrooms

Boiling water

Ground black pepper

1 teaspoon grated fresh ginger

1 tablespoon vegan fish sauce, such as 24Vegan

1 tablespoon toasted sesame oil

¼ cup (60 ml) dark soy sauce

1 tablespoon vegan oyster sauce, such as Lee Kum Kee

Neutral oil, for frying

½ cup (60 g) thinly sliced carrot

½ cup (25 g) baby corn

1 medium red onion, coarsely chopped

½ red bell pepper, sliced

1 tablespoon cornstarch

1 scallion, sliced

2 cups (350 g) steamed white basmati rice

1 vegan fried egg, such as Yo Egg sunny-side up egg (see Note, page 74)

Satini Cotomili (Cilantro Chutney; page 220), Piment Crazée (Mauritian Chile Garlic Paste; page 221), and/or Satini Coco (Coconut Chutney; page 222), for serving

In a heatproof bowl, soak the mushrooms in boiling water to cover. Allow them to sit for 15 minutes, then drain and squeeze out any excess water with your hands. Thinly slice the mushrooms and set them aside.

In a bowl, combine the black pepper, grated ginger, fish sauce, sesame oil, dark soy sauce, and oyster sauce. Add the mushrooms into the mixture and let marinate for 10 minutes.

In a wok or any large nonstick pan, heat 2 tablespoons oil over high heat. Remove the mushrooms from the marinade, reserving the sauce. Sauté the mushrooms for 5 minutes, until slightly browned. Set aside.

Wipe out your pan and then heat 2 tablespoons oil over high heat. Throw in the carrot, baby corn, red onion, and bell pepper, plus the remainder of the marinade from the mushrooms. Stir well and sauté for 5 minutes.

In a small bowl, mix the cornstarch with 3 tablespoons water to form a cornstarch slurry.

Continued

Bol Renversé (Magic Bowl) CONTINUED

Add ¼ cup (60 ml) water and the cornstarch slurry to the wok. Cook until the sauce thickens, about 2 minutes. Add the scallion, stir briefly, then take off the heat.

Fill a bowl 8 inches (20 cm) in diameter halfway with the stir-fried vegetables, spreading into an even layer. Next, spread a layer of rice, filling the bowl completely. Press down firmly to pack everything well. Set the bowl aside.

In a small nonstick pan, heat oil over medium heat and fry the vegan egg for 3 minutes.

Place a plate over the bowl and turn it upside down. Remove the bowl to reveal the bol renversé. Top with the fried egg and serve with your preferred condiments.

NOTE

Instead of a vegan fried egg, you could make a small omelet with some JUST Egg. But I would highly suggest purchasing Yo Egg, as the runny vegan yolk is incredible.

Green Curry with Tofu Fish, Eggplant, and Rice Cakes

SERVES 4 TO 6

Fish curries are a favorite in Mauritius, inspiring me to create this tantalizing dish that boasts the briny and umami-rich flavors that I love with the help of vegan fish sauce and fish paste.

In Mauritius, sweet rice cakes known as idli are a treat enjoyed by many. However, for this dish I recommend the savory idli favored in South India. The soft, fluffy steamed lentil and rice cakes pair perfectly with the aromatic and spicy green curry, and bite-sized servings are a fun way to serve the curry. I like to save time and buy the idli, but if you can't find them at your local Indian grocer, then use my foolproof recipe.

This curry is incredibly versatile. Serving it with a bowl of steamy hot rice allows the rich flavors to meld beautifully. To take it up a notch, add my Satini Cotomili (Cilantro Chutney; page 220) for an extra layer of depth and flavor.

- 1 (14-ounce/397 g) package extra-firm tofu
- 2 tablespoons Old Bay seasoning
- ¼ cup (30 g) cornstarch
- 4 tablespoons (60 ml) neutral oil
- 1 medium white onion, thinly sliced
- ½ teaspoon fenugreek powder
- 1 tablespoon fresh thyme leaves, chopped
- 6 fresh curry leaves
- 3 tablespoons green curry powder
- ¼ cup (60 ml) warm water
- 2 tomatoes, finely diced
- 1 teaspoon grated fresh ginger
- 1 teaspoon store-bought garlic paste
- 1 tablespoon vegan fish sauce, such as 24Vegan
- 1 tablespoon vegan shrimp paste, such as Red Lotus (see Note)
- 2 cups (480 ml) canned unsweetened coconut milk
- 4 eggplants, diced (I use 2 Thai and 2 Indian eggplants)
- 12 idlis (rice cakes), homemade (page 77) or frozen
- Unsweetened shredded coconut, for garnish
- ½ cup (10 g) fresh spinach leaves

Drain the tofu, pat dry, and cut into ½-inch (12 mm) dice.

In a large bowl, combine the Old Bay and cornstarch. Add the tofu cubes and toss to coat them in the mixture.

In a large skillet, heat 2 tablespoons of the oil over medium heat. Add the tofu and fry until crispy and golden brown on all sides, flipping halfway through, about 3 minutes per side. Remove from the pan and set aside.

In the same skillet, heat the remaining 2 tablespoons of oil over medium heat. Add the onion, fenugreek powder, thyme, and curry leaves and cook for 2 minutes.

In a small bowl, combine the green curry powder and warm water to form a paste.

Add the curry paste to the onion-herb mixture and stir to combine. Add the tomatoes, grated ginger, garlic paste, fish sauce, shrimp paste, and coconut milk. Cover and cook on medium heat until the tomatoes are tender, about 15 minutes. If it looks dry, add enough water to maintain a saucy consistency.

Add the fried tofu and the eggplants and simmer, covered, for 10 minutes.

Meanwhile, steam the idlis according to the package instructions (or per the recipe on page 77).

To serve, arrange the rice cakes on a large plate. Cover each rice cake with a few spinach leaves, a spoonful of curry, a teaspoon of chutney, and a sprinkle of coconut.

NOTE

SWAP OPTION: If you can't find vegan shrimp paste, use red miso—you will still achieve a tasty result.

Homemade Idlis (Soft Rice Cakes)

MAKES 20 RICE CAKES

If you can't find frozen idlis or just want to try making them from scratch, this fuss-free recipe skips the hassle of grinding rice.

½ cup (95 g) urad dal (split black lentils)

½ tablespoon fenugreek seeds

2 tablespoons steamed white basmati rice

1½ cups (220 g) white rice flour, such as Bob's Red Mill

Salt

Neutral oil

EQUIPMENT:

Food processor

Idli molds (see Note)

In a bowl, soak the urad dal and fenugreek seeds in water to cover for 4 to 6 hours.

Drain the soaked dal and seeds, then add them, the cooked rice, and 1¼ cups (300 ml) water to a food processor and process until smooth.

Transfer the batter to a mixing bowl. Add the rice flour and a pinch of salt and mix well to combine. Cover the bowl and let the batter ferment in a warm place for 8 hours. It will become slightly airy and frothy with a light, bubbly texture and tangy aroma. The batter should have a smoother, lighter consistency compared to before fermentation. It may expand and appear a bit thicker and more voluminous. This is a sign that the fermentation process is working and the batter is ready to be steamed into idlis.

After fermentation, add more salt to taste and mix gently.

Fill a large pot with enough water so that the water will not touch the bottommost idli mold and bring to a simmer.

Grease the molds with a little oil. Pour the batter into the molds so they are almost full but not overflowing, place the molds into the pot, cover the pot with a lid, and allow the idli to steam for 15 minutes over medium-high heat, until the batter is cooked through and a toothpick inserted in the center of a cake comes out clean.

Once the idlis are done, gently splash a bit of water on the back plate of the idli mold, making sure not to get any water directly on the idlis, to help loosen the cakes from the mold.

Carefully remove the idli from the molds. Use a spoon to gently loosen the edges from the sides of the mold and then turn the mold over and tap the idli out. Serve immediately.

NOTE

You can buy idli molds online (they usually come with a stand that can make several idli at once). Or simply use small heat-resistant glass bowls 2 to 3 inches (5 to 7.5 cm) in diameter, setting them on a metal rack in the pot so the bowls do not touch the simmering water.

Mine Frire (Mauritian Fried Noodles)

SERVES 2

In Mauritius, we're crazy about fried noodles—an easy, go-to dish that's like a flavor bomb in a wok. Stir-fried chow mein noodles are jazzed up with dark soy sauce and vegan fish sauce.

This recipe is an absolute lifesaver on those busy days when you want something tasty but don't have hours to spend in the kitchen. What's cool is that you can make it your own. Any veggies hanging around? Chuck 'em in!

Trust me, when the wok starts to sizzle and the smells start to swirl, you'll know something good is happening. It's comfort food at its finest, Mauritian style.

- 10 ounces (300 g) egg-free chow mein noodles
- 1 tablespoon plus 2 teaspoons toasted sesame oil
- ½ cup (120 ml) JUST Egg (optional)
- 1 teaspoon unsalted plant-based butter, such as Earth Balance, for cooking the egg (optional)
- Neutral oil, for frying
- 2 cloves garlic, minced
- 1 (1½-inch/4 cm) piece fresh ginger, peeled and minced
- 2 cups (220 g) shredded carrots
- 2 cups (190 g) shredded white cabbage
- 1 sweet red pepper, thinly sliced
- 2 green chiles, sliced in half lengthwise
- ¼ cup (11 g) sliced garlic chives
- 2 tablespoons dark soy sauce
- ¼ cup (60 ml) vegan oyster sauce, such as Lee Kum Kee
- 4 teaspoons vegan fish sauce
- 2 teaspoons rice wine vinegar
- Ground black pepper
- 1 cup (70 g) chopped bok choy
- 1 scallion, sliced on a bias
- 2 teaspoons Piment Crazée (Mauritian Chile Garlic Paste; page 221), plus more for garnish (optional)
- Satini Cotomili (Cilantro Chutney; page 220), for garnish (optional)

Cook the noodles per the instructions on the packet. Once done, give them a good rinse with cold water and add 1 tablespoon sesame oil to keep them from sticking together.

If adding vegan egg to your noodles, in a medium nonstick pan, melt the butter. Pour in the JUST Egg and cook until it sets, then flip to cook the other side. Cut the omelet into thin 1-inch (2.5 cm) strips and set them aside.

In a wok, heat a thin layer of neutral oil over high heat. Add the garlic and ginger and stir constantly for about 1 minute, ensuring the garlic doesn't burn.

Toss in the carrots, cabbage, sweet red pepper, green chiles, and chives, reserving 1 teaspoon of the chives for garnish. Sauté this veggie medley for about 1 minute.

Add the cooked noodles to the wok, then drizzle in the dark soy sauce, oyster sauce, fish sauce, vinegar, and a dash of pepper, and the remaining 2 teaspoons sesame oil. Continue sautéing for a few minutes, until everything is well coated and heated through.

Add the bok choy, scallion, and the piment crazée, if using, to the mix and sauté for about 5 minutes, ensuring the veggies are well coated in the sauce and are heated through but still maintain a delightful crunch.

Toward the end, sprinkle in the reserved chives and add the strips of omelet, if using.

If you're feeling a bit spicy, add another dollop of piment crazée and a drizzle of satini cotomili for an extra kick!

NOTE

PROTEIN POWER: Consider adding vegan shrimp, chicken, crispy fried tofu, or any other plant-based protein you love.

Rougaille Saucisse (Sausages in Tomato Sauce)

SERVES 4

Rougaille saucisse is a beloved dish in Mauritius that combines sausages with a rich tomato sauce that is infused with a blend of African, Indian, and French influences. This laid-back dish takes center stage at family dinners, putting a smile on everyone's face. As a kid, I practically lived on rougaille saucisse, enjoying it at least twice a week.

Vegan sausages have come a long way and have allowed me to re-create this dish with all its flavors intact. It's amazing how these plant-based alternatives can capture the essence of the original dish while being cruelty-free and environmentally friendly. Now everyone can enjoy the comforting goodness of rougaille saucisse!

6 plant-based sausages (see Note)

Neutral oil, for frying

6 cups (1.4 L) Rougaille Sauce (page 133)

Steamed white basmati rice, for serving

Chopped fresh cilantro, for garnish (optional)

Green chiles, for garnish (optional)

Slice the sausages into ¾-inch (2 cm) pieces.

In a large pan, heat a thin layer of oil over medium-high heat. Add the sausages and fry the pieces, turning occasionally, until they're golden brown on all sides. Once done, remove the sausages from the pan and set them aside to cool slightly.

Meanwhile, in a medium saucepan, bring the rougaille to a simmer. Add the fried sausages to the sauce. Let them hang out together and simmer on low heat for 10 to 15 minutes, allowing all those flavors to mix and mingle.

Once everything is perfectly infused, serve the rougaille saucisse over rice. Give it a finishing touch by garnishing with fresh cilantro or green chiles, if using.

Jerk Mushroom Tacos

SERVES 2

As soon as you land in Jamaica and hit the road from the airport, the irresistible, smoky scent of jerk chicken and pork grilling in massive barbecue drums beckons you to pull over. It's a practically a magnetic force!

Jerk, for those unfamiliar, is a traditional Jamaican cooking style that involves marinating meat or vegetables in a blend of seasonings, including Scotch bonnet peppers, allspice, thyme, and various other spices. The marinated food is then grilled or smoked over pimento wood.

I've taken that Jamaican classic and given it a vegan makeover. These mushrooms are a tantalizing delight that pays homage to the culinary heritage of Jamaica. Adding my own flair to the mix, I've turned this into a taco filling and added my Mauritian mango chutney for a burst of sweet and tangy goodness that takes this dish to a whole new level that's nothing short of absolute fire!

FOR THE MARINADE:

2 Scotch bonnet peppers, seeded and halved

1 shallot, chopped

3 scallions, chopped

4 cloves garlic, halved

3 tablespoons coconut brown sugar

3 tablespoons apple cider vinegar

3 tablespoons soy sauce or tamari

2 tablespoons neutral oil

1 (1-inch/2.5 cm) piece fresh ginger, peeled and coarsely chopped

1 tablespoon ground allspice

1 teaspoon ground nutmeg

1 teaspoon fresh thyme leaves

½ teaspoon ground cinnamon

½ teaspoon salt

14 ounces (400 g) king oyster mushrooms

FOR THE COLESLAW:

⅔ cup (158 ml) vegan mayonnaise, such as Hellmann's

2 tablespoons apple cider vinegar

1 tablespoon Dijon mustard

1 teaspoon coconut brown sugar

Salt and ground black pepper

3 cups (285 g) shredded green cabbage

1 cup (95 g) shredded red cabbage

½ cup (55 g) shredded carrots

FOR SERVING:

Neutral oil, for cooking

8 small, soft flour tortillas

Juice of 2 limes

1 bunch fresh cilantro

Mango Satini (Mango Chutney; page 224)

TO MARINATE THE MUSHROOMS:

To a blender, add the Scotch bonnet peppers, shallot, scallions, garlic, brown sugar, vinegar, soy sauce, oil, ginger, allspice, nutmeg, thyme, cinnamon, and salt and blend for 2 to 3 minutes or until smooth.

Use a fork to shred the oyster mushrooms, then pull the individual strands apart with your hands. Place the mushrooms in a bowl.

Pour the jerk marinade over the mushrooms and toss to coat. Cover and refrigerate for at least 1 hour, but ideally overnight.

TO MAKE THE COLESLAW:

In a small bowl, whisk the mayo, vinegar, mustard, brown sugar, salt, and black pepper.

In a very large mixing bowl (the larger, the better), combine the cabbage and carrots.

Pour the dressing all over the green and red cabbage and carrots and toss well to combine. Finish with more salt and black pepper to taste. The coleslaw can be prepared in advance and stored in a glass container in the refrigerator for up to 2 days.

TO COOK THE MUSHROOMS AND SERVE:

In a medium frying pan, heat a thin layer of oil over medium-high heat. When the oil is hot, add the marinated mushrooms and cook, flipping frequently, until the edges of the mushrooms crisp up, approximately 5 minutes.

Fill each of the tortillas with jerk mushrooms, coleslaw, a drizzle of lime juice, some cilantro, and mango chutney.

Green Banana Rundown

SERVES 6

Rundown is a famous stew from Jamaica. Forget every stew you have ever tried before—this one is in a league of its own. Coconut milk, spices, and other ingredients such as seafood (often salted mackerel) and vegetables are slowly cooked together until the coconut milk reduces and thickens, transforming into a luscious sauce. This slow simmering process may have given this stew its name.

In my version, I use green bananas instead of fish, as green bananas are a great source of protein and really soak up the sauce well. My uncle in Jamaica, who is a Rasta, uses green bananas in his rundown, reflecting the Ital way of living, which is about not consuming animals. Jamaican green bananas taste starchy and mildly bitter, with a texture that is firm and dense. The flavor is more vegetal and less sweet compared to ripe bananas, and when cooked they have a subtle, slightly earthy taste that can be compared to potatoes. The taste is mild, allowing them to complement savory dishes well.

And don't forget to serve the stew with a side of my crispy Fried Bakes (page 129), which are perfect for sopping up all the coconut sauce from the bottom of the pan.

- 5 to 7 medium green (unripe) bananas
- 1 tablespoon refined coconut oil
- 1 medium white onion, chopped
- 3 cloves garlic, finely chopped
- 1 tablespoon grated fresh ginger
- 2 scallions, chopped
- 1 tomato, diced
- 3 sprigs thyme
- 5 pimento berries or ¼ teaspoon ground allspice
- 1 teaspoon Cajun seasoning
- 1 (13½-ounce/400 ml) can unsweetened coconut milk
- 1 red bell pepper, sliced
- 6 fresh curry leaves
- 1 Scotch bonnet pepper
- Salt

Wash the bananas, then trim the stem and blossom ends. Using a sharp knife, make a cut lengthwise through only the skin, along the side of each banana. Peel away the skin from each banana.

In a large pot, bring water to a boil. Add the bananas, reduce the heat to a simmer, and cook until the bananas are tender when pierced with a fork, about 20 minutes. Drain and set aside.

Meanwhile, in a large cast-iron pan over medium-high heat, heat the oil. When the oil is hot, add the white onion and cook until soft, about 2 minutes. Stir in the garlic, ginger, and scallions and cook until fragrant, about 1 minute.

Add the tomato, thyme sprigs, pimento berries, Cajun seasoning, coconut milk, bell pepper, curry leaves, whole Scotch bonnet pepper, and salt to taste.

Add the whole boiled green bananas to the skillet and bring the mixture to a simmer. Cover the pan and let the rundown cook until the sauce thickens, 5 to 8 minutes. Remove the sprigs of thyme and serve immediately.

Tofu Vindaye

SERVES 4

Vindaye holds a special place in Mauritian history, tracing its roots back to the Portuguese phrase *vinha d'alhos*, meaning "wine and garlic." From Portugal, the phrase traveled to India, where it became the renowned curry vindaloo before finally gracing the vibrant kitchens of Mauritius.

In Mauritius, vindaye evolved into a unique curry traditionally made with spicy pickled fish and local ingredients like turmeric, mustard seeds, onions, and vinegar. Its tangy and aromatic flavors have made it a favorite among locals and visitors alike, representing the melding of Indian, African, Chinese, and European culinary influences that defines Mauritian cuisine.

In this recipe, we reimagine the traditional vindaye using tofu as a delicious vegan alternative to fish. Tofu's ability to absorb flavors makes it a perfect canvas for the bold essence of vindaye. Typically served in a fresh bread roll or baguette, this sandwich combines the zesty and spicy vindaye—a pickled vegetable dish—with the simplicity of the bread.

Join me in celebrating Mauritian heritage with a modern twist that's sure to delight your taste buds.

- 2 (14-ounce/397 g) packs extra-firm tofu
- 2 tablespoons coarsely ground black mustard seeds
- 2 tablespoons ground turmeric
- ¼ teaspoon fenugreek seeds
- 3 tablespoons neutral oil, plus more as needed
- 2 cloves garlic, peeled and cut into strips
- 3 whole green or red chiles, sliced in half lengthwise
- 6 fresh curry leaves, plus more for garnish, if desired
- 2 large red onions or 6 shallots, sliced
- ½ teaspoon salt, plus more as needed
- 3 tablespoons white wine vinegar
- Steamed white basmati rice or warm baguette, for serving

Drain the tofu, pat dry, and cut it into bite-size cubes.

In a small bowl, combine the mustard seeds, turmeric, and fenugreek seeds.

In a medium cast-iron pan over medium-high heat, heat the oil to prepare for tempering. When the oil is hot, add the garlic, whole chiles, and curry leaves. Sauté until aromatic.

Add the spice blend to the pan, stir well, and sauté the mixture for another minute to allow it to temper.

Add the onions and salt to the pan. Cook until the onions are softened and golden, 3 to 4 minutes.

Gently place the tofu cubes into the pan so they do not break. Toss to coat them evenly with the aromatic spice mixture. Pour the vinegar over the tofu.

Fry the tofu until it's brown and slightly crisp. If the vindaye appears dry, add some additional oil.

Plate your vindaye, garnishing with additional curry leaves, if using, and enjoy with rice or a warm baguette.

Vegan Fried Chicken

SERVES 4

In every Jamaican household, there's a secret recipe for battering fried chicken (or mushrooms for those that don't eat meat), but nothing quite compares to my grandma's triple-dipped oyster mushrooms, also affectionately known as Vegan Fried Chicken or VFC. The memories flood back vividly—standing in her kitchen, surrounded by the aromas of culinary magic as she guided me through mixing a huge batch of these delectable treats.

What sets these mushrooms apart? It's all about the coating! I swore to keep the recipe close, but I can't resist sharing a little secret: malt vinegar in the wet batter. It's the key to the perfect balance of flavors and textures, creating a crispy and flavorful coating that's simply unbeatable.

To really bring out the best flavor in your VFC, there's a little trick that makes a big difference: As soon as your mushrooms come out of the hot oil, season them immediately with pepper, salt, or even your favorite spice blend. Doing this while the mushrooms are still sizzling ensures that the seasoning sticks perfectly to their crispy, golden surface. The heat will help the spices bloom, enhancing the overall flavor profile of the dish. This technique also allows you to customize the VFC according to your taste. If you're feeling adventurous, you can try smoked paprika, garlic powder, or even a dash of cayenne for extra heat. The combination of the freshly fried mushrooms and the aromatic spices will elevate the dish to a new level of flavor complexity.

Although Grandma Bernice is no longer with us, her spirit lives on through cherished recipes like this one. Join me in honoring her legacy and savoring the deliciousness of VFC—a true taste of home and heart.

When it comes to serving, make sure to plate the VFC while it's still hot to preserve that irresistible crispiness. Pair it with a cool, crunchy coleslaw for contrast, plus some dipping sauces—classic ketchup for sweetness and hot sauce for a fiery kick. My mac and cheese on page 159 would be another perfect thing to add to your table. But if I'm being honest, you'll start eating the VFC before they even hit your plate!

Continued

Vegan Fried Chicken
CONTINUED

In a high-sided, heavy pot like a Dutch oven, heat 4 inches (10 cm) of oil to 350°F (175°C) when measured with a deep-fry thermometer.

In a medium bowl, combine the oat milk and vinegar to make the wet batter.

In another medium bowl, combine the flour, cornstarch, garlic powder, paprika, onion powder, thyme, pepper, chicken-flavored seasoning, Old Bay, and celery salt to make the seasoned flour.

Pull the oyster mushrooms apart to your desired size—I prefer small, bite-size pieces for optimal crunch, but leaving the mushrooms mostly whole will be juicier.

Dip the mushroom pieces in the seasoned flour. Shake off any excess, then dip the mushrooms in the wet batter, and then dip them in the seasoned flour once more.

Working in batches (see Notes), lower the mushroom pieces carefully into the hot oil. Fry until crispy and well browned, 8 to 10 minutes. Use a spider to transfer the fried mushrooms to a wire rack with a baking sheet underneath or a paper towel–lined plate to drain.

If you want to take the flavor up a notch, season the mushrooms with some extra pepper, salt, or your favorite seasoning mix immediately after they come out of the oil. The spices will stick well to the hot mushrooms.

Serve the VFC while hot, with coleslaw and a few dipping sauces like ketchup and hot sauce, if using.

Neutral oil, for frying (see Notes)

1 cup (240 ml) plain oat milk

¼ cup (60 ml) malt or white vinegar

3 cups (375 g) all-purpose flour

3 tablespoons cornstarch

2 teaspoons garlic powder

2 teaspoons paprika

2 teaspoons onion powder

2 teaspoons dried thyme

2 teaspoons ground black pepper, plus more for finishing (optional)

2 teaspoons vegan chicken-flavored seasoning, such as Grace Chicken Seasoning

2 teaspoons Old Bay seasoning

2 teaspoons celery salt

1 pound (455 g) oyster mushrooms

Salt (optional)

FOR SERVING (OPTIONAL):

Coleslaw (see page 83)

Ketchup

Scotch Bonnet Mango Hot Sauce (page 225)

NOTES

OIL OPTIONS: Use an oil with a high smoke point, such as rice bran, peanut, vegetable, or canola, to prevent the oil from breaking down at high temperatures.

SMALL BATCHES: Fry the oyster mushrooms in modest batches to avoid overcrowding, which helps ensure even cooking and prevents sogginess.

Mauritian Lentil Crepes

MAKES 6 CREPES

These Mauritian crepes are like a cross between Ethiopian injera and South Indian dosa, with a soft texture and slightly tangy flavor. But what really takes these crepes from ordinary to extraordinary are my condiments and sides. Fill these with Rougaille (page 133), some chutneys (pages 220, 222–224), any cooked vegetable (like bitter gourd; page 156), and pickled vegetables (page 137). The beauty of this crepe is its versatility—you can fill it with all of your favorite things, creating a delightful explosion of flavors in every bite. After soaking the lentils, all it takes is a whirlwind in the blender, and voilà, we're in the crepe-making business!

- 1 cup (200 g) split red lentils, rinsed well
- 1 teaspoon salt
- 1 teaspoon baking powder
- 1 teaspoon ground cumin
- 1 teaspoon ground turmeric
- 1 (1-inch/2.5 cm) piece fresh ginger, peeled
- 2 cloves garlic
- 1 tablespoon apple cider vinegar
- Handful fresh cilantro
- 2 green chiles
- Neutral oil, for frying

Preheat the oven to 200°F (90°C).

Place the lentils in a heatproof bowl. Pour boiling water over them to cover completely. Soak the lentils for at least 3 hours or overnight, then drain and rinse them well.

To a food processor, add the lentils, salt, baking powder, cumin, turmeric, ginger, garlic, vinegar, cilantro, chiles, and 1 cup (240 ml) water and blitz to a creamy batter (see Note).

Heat a 10-inch (25 cm) nonstick frying pan over medium heat. Brush the pan with a little oil.

Ladle ¼ cup (60 ml) batter into the pan and tilt the pan in a circular motion so that the batter coats the surface evenly. Allow the crepe to cook for 2 to 3 minutes, until it bubbles and comes away easily at the edge. Flip the crepe using a spatula and cook the other side for about 1 minute, until that side easily releases from the bottom of the pan. Transfer the crepe to a baking sheet and place in the oven to keep warm. Repeat with the remaining batter, brushing the pan with more oil as needed between batches.

Serve the crepes warm.

NOTE

TEXTURE VARIATION: Grind the batter to your desired consistency, opting for a smooth paste for a softer texture or a coarser grind for added bite.

London

FOR THE VEGAN FISH AND THE BATTER:

- 1 (18-ounce/510 g) can banana blossoms
- 4 snack-size sheets nori, shredded
- 1 tablespoon kelp powder
- 1 tablespoon vegan fish sauce, such as 24Vegan (optional)
- ⅓ cup (45 g) cornstarch
- 1 snack-size pack nori sheets
- ¼ cup (30 g) all-purpose flour, plus extra for coating
- 2 tablespoons rice flour
- 1 teaspoon celery salt
- Pinch of garlic powder
- 1 teaspoon paprika
- 1 teaspoon baking powder
- ½ cup (120 ml) sparkling water, ice cold
- Neutral oil, for frying
- Cornichons

FOR THE TARTAR SAUCE:

- ½ cup (120 ml) vegan mayonnaise, such as Hellmann's
- 4 teaspoons finely chopped capers
- 4 teaspoons finely chopped dill pickles or cornichons, plus more whole pickles for serving
- 4 teaspoons finely chopped fresh parsley
- Lemon juice

FOR THE CHIPS:

- 4½ pounds (2 kg) starchy potatoes, such as Idaho Russet, Maris Piper, or King Edward
- Neutral oil, for frying
- Salt

TO PREPARE THE VEGAN FISH AND THE BATTER:

Drain and rinse the banana blossoms. Gently press the banana blossoms to flatten them into filet-like shapes. Be careful, as they are delicate and can tear easily. Place the banana blossoms on a clean kitchen towel and cover with another towel. Gently press and squeeze to remove as much liquid as possible without breaking them. This step is crucial to help them to absorb the marinade and avoid splatters.

In a mixing bowl, whisk together the nori, kelp powder, and fish sauce, if using. Add the banana blossoms, then cover the bowl and place it in the freezer for 1 hour.

In a large bowl, whisk together the cornstarch, all-purpose flour, rice flour, celery salt, garlic powder, paprika, and baking powder. Gradually add the sparkling water while continuing to whisk to create a smooth batter until just combined. It should have the consistency of pancake batter; you may not need all the sparkling water. Be careful not to overmix the batter! Set aside.

TO MAKE THE TARTAR SAUCE:

In a small bowl, combine the mayonnaise, capers, pickles, and parsley. Add a squeeze of lemon juice and mix to combine.

TO FRY THE CHIPS AND FISH, AND TO SERVE:

Peel and cut the potatoes into thick batons. Traditional chip-shop chips are much wider than standard French fries, so aim for pieces about 1 inch (2.5 cm) wide and ½ inch (12 mm) thick. Soak the cut potatoes in cool water for at least 30 minutes. This helps to remove excess starch to achieve a crispier finish.

Continued

After soaking, rinse the potatoes thoroughly under cold water and pat them dry with a clean kitchen towel or paper towels.

In a deep, heavy-bottomed pot, heat 4 inches (10 cm) oil to 250 to 265°F (120 to 130°C) when measured with a deep-fry thermometer. If you don't have a deep-fry thermometer, test the temperature by adding a small piece of potato; it should bubble gently (see Note).

Fry the potatoes in batches for the first time briefly, 5 to 7 minutes, just to blanch them. They should be soft and cooked through, but not colored. Using a spider, remove the chips and drain them on a rack or paper towels. Turn off the heat but save your pot of frying oil, as we'll be using it again later.

Let the blanched chips cool to room temperature. This step is crucial, as it allows the interior of the chips to settle.

Meanwhile, batter the banana blossoms: Gently separate the layers of the chilled banana blossoms. To create a fish-like texture and taste, cut the nori sheets to the size of each layer and place a sheet of nori between each layer. This will help infuse the banana blossoms with that desired oceanic flavor.

Add the flour to a shallow bowl. Toss the banana blossoms in the flour to coat them, getting in all the crevices.

Dunk the floured blossoms in the batter, leaving a thick coating.

You need to fry the banana blossoms and the chips for a second time simultaneously but in separate pots, so prepare a second pot of frying oil for the blossoms: In a large, tall-sided pot, add about 1 inch (2.5 cm) of oil, making sure it doesn't reach more than halfway up the sides of the pan. Heat until the temperature reaches around 350°F (175°C).

When the chips have cooled, fry the chips for a second time: Reheat the oil in the pot used to fry the chips previously, until the oil temperature reaches 350 to 375°F (175 to 190°C). Fry the chips in batches for 5 to 7 minutes, until golden and crisp. Drain the chips well on a rack or paper towels and sprinkle them with salt.

At the same time as frying the chips, in your second pot of hot oil (see Note), fry the blossoms until crisp, about 3 minutes per side, flipping halfway. They won't get super golden brown, but make sure you turn them so they fry evenly. Remove them from the oil and drain on a paper towel.

Arrange the fried banana blossoms on a platter and serve with the chips, tartar sauce, and some cornichons.

NOTE

TEMPERATURE CHECK: Keep an eye on the oil temperature. You may need to adjust the heat when you add food to the oil. A thermometer is handy.

Bouillon Cresson (Watercress Broth) with Crispy Lion's Mane Mushrooms

SERVES 2

This simple, nourishing broth is a cherished Mauritian comfort food that means so much to me, reminding me of my childhood in East London. It warms my heart that this is now my daughter's favorite dish.

Traditionally, it's served with fish rougaille—crispy pieces of fish in a rich tomato sauce. Taking inspiration from the crispiness of fish rougaille, I'm topping this broth with crispy lion's mane mushroom instead, along with a spoonful of plain tomato rougaille.

Jump on over to the condiments section and pair this with my Mauritian Chile Garlic Paste (page 221), or my cilantro (page 220), coconut (page 222), or green mango (page 223) chutneys.

FOR THE CRISPY LION'S MANE MUSHROOMS:

- 8 ounces (225 g) lion's mane mushrooms
- 1 tablespoon olive oil
- 1 teaspoon celery salt
- ¼ teaspoon ground black pepper
- 1 teaspoon smoked paprika
- ½ teaspoon mustard powder
- ¼ teaspoon ground allspice
- ⅛ teaspoon ground cloves
- ⅛ teaspoon ground ginger
- ⅛ teaspoon cayenne pepper

FOR THE WATERCRESS BROTH AND SERVING:

- 2 cups (480 ml) Rougaille Sauce (page 133)
- Neutral oil
- ½ red onion, sliced
- 6 cups (1.4 L) boiling water
- 1 (1-inch/2.5 cm) piece fresh ginger, peeled and julienned
- 1 cube vegetable stock
- 2 (8-ounce/225 g) packs watercress, cleaned thoroughly
- Steamed white basmati rice

TO PREPARE THE CRISPY LION'S MANE MUSHROOMS:

Shred the mushrooms into bite-size pieces, keeping them a little larger than the desired final size, as they will shrink when cooked.

In a medium skillet, heat the olive oil over medium-high heat and add the shredded mushrooms. Sauté for about 6 minutes, or until the mushrooms are crispy and browned.

Add the celery salt, black pepper, paprika, mustard powder, allspice, cloves, ginger, and cayenne to the skillet. Stir well and cook for an additional 2 minutes. This allows the spices to bloom and the mushrooms to crisp. Set aside.

TO MAKE THE WATERCRESS BROTH AND SERVE:

In a medium pot over medium-high heat, bring the rougaille sauce to a simmer.

In a deep pot, heat a splash of oil over medium heat. Add the onion and sauté for 6 to 8 minutes, until translucent. Add the boiling water, julienned ginger, and vegetable stock cube and stir to combine. Gently add the watercress. Do not cover the pot, as it may cause the leaves to turn yellow.

Take the rougaille sauce off the heat and set aside.

Serve the watercress broth with plain white rice, topped with the rougaille and crispy lion's mane.

Touffer Haricots Verts à la Mauricienne (Sautéed French Beans with Potatoes)

SERVES 4

This traditional Mauritian dish transports me back to the comforting embrace of mealtime at my family home. There's something beautiful about its simplicity. The sautéed beans and potatoes, perfectly seasoned and cooked to perfection, highlight the flavors and essence of Mauritian culinary traditions.

We usually serve this dish alongside piping hot rice and a dollop of one of my Mauritian chutneys (pages 220, 222–224). This meal will fill your stomach and nourish your soul, reminding you that sometimes, it's the simple dishes that leave the most lasting impressions.

- ¼ cup (60 ml) neutral oil
- 1 Yukon Gold potato, peeled and cubed
- 2 or 3 dried red chiles
- 1 medium red onion, sliced
- 4 to 5 cups (380 to 475 g) French green beans, halved lengthwise
- Salt

In a frying pan, heat the oil over medium heat. Add the potato and fry until a little more than half-cooked.

Keeping the potatoes in the pan, drain most of the oil from the pan, leaving around 2 tablespoons. Add the chiles and onion to the pan and sauté for 5 minutes, until the onion is translucent.

Add the halved green beans to the pan. Sprinkle with 2 or 3 pinches of salt and sauté for 2 minutes.

Add ½ cup (120 ml) water and cover the pan. Let it cook until the water is fully evaporated, ensuring the green beans reach your preferred level of tenderness (add more water if you would like them more done). Season with salt to taste and serve.

Mauritian Butter Bean Soup

SERVES 4

Ready to whip up something utterly delicious, but feel like taking it kinda easy? I've got you covered with this no-fuss Mauritian butter bean (also known as lima bean) soup. Trust me, it's a total winner at my table every time. Forget about the hassle of soaking beans overnight: we're keeping it chill with canned beans. Just crack open a can, give those beans a quick rinse, and you're practically halfway there.

Now, the real secret is to pour a little love into the pot and get those island spices just right. That's what transforms a simple meal into "Oh, wow, this is amazing!" You can sip this soup alone, dive in with fresh bread, or pair it with rice and your favorite hearty curry, such as my No Shrimp Curry (page 107). After all, no Mauritian meal is complete without several small dishes on the table!

- 2 tablespoons neutral oil
- 6 fresh curry leaves
- 2 tomatoes, diced
- 1 medium red onion, sliced
- 2 sprigs thyme
- 1 teaspoon minced fresh ginger
- 1 teaspoon minced garlic
- 1 teaspoon salt, plus more as needed
- 1 teaspoon ground coriander
- 1 teaspoon ground cumin
- ¼ teaspoon fenugreek seeds
- ¼ teaspoon fennel seeds
- 2 (15.5-ounce/439 g) cans butter beans, drained (see Note)
- Fresh whole cilantro leaves, for garnish

In a medium pot over medium heat, heat the oil to prepare for tempering. When the oil is hot, add in the curry leaves and allow them to sizzle for 15 seconds.

Add the tomatoes, onion, thyme, ginger, garlic, salt, coriander, cumin, fenugreek seeds, fennel seeds, and ½ cup (120 ml) water. Let the flavors mingle for 5 minutes, stirring occasionally.

Add the beans. Cover and let simmer for 15 minutes. If the soup gets too thick, add some extra water.

Season with salt to taste, garnish with cilantro, remove the thyme sprigs, and serve.

NOTE

You can also use dried beans. Simply follow these guidelines:

Soak 2½ cups (500 g) dried butter beans in room-temperature water for 2 to 3 hours.

Drain the beans and place them in a pressure cooker.

Add 1 teaspoon salt and 5 cups (1.2 L) water.

Pressure-cook on medium-high for approximately 20 minutes. Once the pressure has released, check if the beans are cooked through. They should be soft. If they're not soft enough for your taste, pop the lid back on and steam a little longer

CLOCKWISE FROM TOP: Mango Satini (Mango Chutney; page 224), cilantro, Touffer Haricots Verts à la Mauricienne (page 100), Mauritian Butter Bean Soup (page 101), and One-Pot Pumpkin Soup (page 103).

One-Pot Pumpkin Soup

SERVES 4

I love keeping things simple and laid-back in the kitchen, and that's exactly what this pumpkin soup is all about. It's an ode to eating colorful: just throw in some vibrant veggies, let them swim in a coconut-infused broth, and watch the magic happen.

Mauritians and Jamaicans both make a mean pumpkin soup, so I combined the best of both worlds in this recipe. Yams, carrots, and cabbage make this a very hearty and filling soup that can serve as a meal all by itself. For a finishing touch, a dash of my Scotch Bonnet Mango Hot Sauce (page 225) adds just the right amount of heat and flavor.

2 tablespoons neutral oil

1 large red onion, roughly chopped

½ tablespoon minced fresh ginger

1 teaspoon minced garlic

1 fresh green chile, minced

2 ribs celery, chopped

2 scallions, chopped, plus more for garnish

1 small white yam, peeled and cubed

⅓ small to medium pumpkin, peeled and cubed

2 medium carrots, cut into rounds

2 cobs corn, each cob cut into 6 or 8 pieces

⅓ cup (30 g) thinly shredded cabbage

2 cups (480 ml) vegetable stock

1 teaspoon ground cumin

¼ teaspoon ground turmeric

Salt

¾ teaspoon ground nutmeg

½ cup (120 ml) canned unsweetened coconut milk

Fresh whole curry leaves, for garnish

Fresh whole cilantro leaves, for garnish (optional)

In a large pot, heat the oil over medium heat. Add the red onion, ginger, garlic, and chile and sauté 5 to 7 minutes, until soft and fragrant.

Add the celery, scallions, yam, pumpkin, carrots, corn, and cabbage. Sauté for about 5 minutes.

Pour in the vegetable stock. Add the cumin, turmeric, and season with salt to taste. Bring to a boil, then reduce the heat and simmer for 20 minutes, until the vegetables are tender.

Stir in the nutmeg, then add the coconut milk. Remove the soup from the heat and ladle it into individual serving bowls. Serve hot, garnished with scallions, curry leaves, and fresh cilantro, if using.

Back in the day, I loved to savor chicken kebabs from my favorite Indian spot on Brick Lane in East London! Nostalgia for those kebabs has hit me hard since going vegan, so I decided to re-create them in all their glory! The seasonings for the tikka marinade are all the spices we use in Mauritius, blending the robust flavors of turmeric, cumin, and garam masala—staples we share with Indian cuisines. I guarantee your guests will devour these, savoring each bite as a celebration of cultural heritage and culinary innovation.

1 cup (240 ml) unsweetened plain plant-based yogurt

3 tablespoons tomato paste

2 tablespoons olive oil

6 cloves garlic, minced

1 tablespoon minced fresh ginger

2 tablespoons fresh lemon juice

2 teaspoons garam masala

1 teaspoon paprika

1 teaspoon cumin

1 teaspoon salt

½ teaspoon ground turmeric

½ teaspoon chili powder

½ teaspoon Himalayan black salt (for a salty, earthy flavor)

¼ teaspoon cayenne pepper

1 (14-ounce/397 g) package extra-firm tofu

Chopped fresh cilantro, for garnish

Steamed white basmati rice, for serving

Lemon wedges, for serving

Satini Cotomili (Cilantro Chutney; page 220), for serving

EQUIPMENT:

Wooden or metal skewers (see Notes)

In a large mixing bowl, whisk together the yogurt, tomato paste, olive oil, garlic, ginger, lemon juice, garam masala, paprika, cumin, salt, turmeric, chili powder, black salt, and cayenne.

Drain the tofu well and pat it completely dry with a paper towel, removing as much moisture as possible. This will help the tofu hold its shape. Then, slice the tofu into 1-inch (25 mm) cubes.

Toss the tofu with the spice mixture until each piece is well coated. Transfer the tofu and spice mixture to an airtight container and refrigerate for at least 2 hours, or overnight (see Notes).

Preheat the oven to 450°F (230°C).

Remove the tofu from the refrigerator, give it a toss to recoat the tofu, then thread the tofu onto skewers. Reserve any remaining marinade.

Line a 16 by 12–inch (40.5 by 30.5 cm) baking pan with foil. Balance the skewers on the baking dish rims so that the tofu is suspended over the pan. Space the skewers so the tofu does not touch.

Bake for 15 minutes, until the tofu starts to brown in spots. Remove the dish from the oven, brush the tofu with any remaining marinade, flip each skewer, and return the dish to the oven to bake for an additional 10 minutes, until the tofu begins to brown in spots again.

Set the pan under the broiler for the last minute or two to obtain a char reminiscent of tandoor cooking. Keep an eye on the skewers, as they can burn very quickly!

Remove the skewers from the oven and sprinkle with chopped cilantro. Serve immediately with rice, lemon wedges, and satini cotomili.

NOTES

MARINATION TIME: Marinating the tofu for longer enhances flavor penetration. For maximum flavor, consider marinating the tofu overnight, if time allows.

SOAK FIRST: To prevent wooden skewers from catching fire while grilling, soak them in cool water for at least 30 minutes before loading them up.

No Shrimp Curry

SERVES 2

Mauritian curries are distinguished from curries in other global cuisines by their drier consistency and concentrated flavor. In traditional Mauritian shrimp curry, for example, the shrimp are enveloped in a rich, spiced coating rather than swimming in a heavy sauce.

For a while after I became vegan, I reckoned that the pleasure of savoring a shrimp curry was a thing of the past for me—until I discovered the groundbreaking innovation by Cavi-art, a visionary enterprise from Denmark. Since their inception in 1988, they have been at the forefront of culinary innovation, led by biologist Jens Møller. It began with a simple basement experiment with seaweed meant to entertain his children. After many iterations, numerous sleepless nights, and endless taste tests, Møller created a vegan caviar alternative that has utterly enchanted me. But he didn't stop there—just when I thought it couldn't possibly get any better, Cavi-art unveiled vegan shrimp!

You can serve this curry on its own, or with homemade chapatis (page 153) or Pilau Rice (page 149), and of course Creole condiments are a must: Satini Coco (Coconut Chutney; page 222), Satini Mangue Vert (Green Mango Chutney; page 223), and Satini Cotomili (Cilantro Chutney; page 220).

- 2 tablespoons lemon juice
- 1 teaspoon Homemade Mauritian Curry Powder (page 231)
- 1 teaspoon salt, plus more as needed
- 1 pound (455 g) vegan shrimp, such as Cavi-art or All Vegetarian
- 1 tablespoon unrefined coconut oil
- 1 large red onion, chopped
- 10 fresh curry leaves
- 1 tablespoon grated fresh ginger
- 1 tablespoon store-bought garlic paste
- 1 cup (40 g) chopped fresh cilantro, plus more for garnish
- 1 tomato, finely chopped

In a large bowl, combine the lemon juice, curry powder, ½ teaspoon of the salt, and the shrimp and mix well. Set aside to marinate while you prepare the rest of the dish.

In a large, cast-iron pan over medium-high heat, heat the oil to prepare for tempering. When the oil is hot, add the onion and sauté for 4 to 6 minutes, until browned. Add the curry leaves, then add the grated ginger, garlic paste, cilantro, and remaining ½ teaspoon salt. Cook, stirring, for 1 minute.

Mix in the tomato, the marinated shrimp, and ¼ cup (60 ml) water. Reduce the heat to medium and cook for 7 to 8 minutes.

Taste and adjust salt if necessary. Remove from the heat, garnish with more fresh cilantro, and serve.

East London Kebab Shop Gyro

SERVES 4

Oh, how I recall those wild Friday nights in East London! After hitting the town with my girls, nothing would beat our craving for a kebab, gyro, or shawarma. Cumin, coriander, chili, garlic—bold, spicy flavors that take me back.

On *The Black Vegan Cooking Show*, I got to bring the magic of East London kebab shops right into award-winning rapper and record executive Jim Jones's kitchen. He couldn't even tell that these gyros were vegan! I want to help you create the same experience right at home.

1 pound (455 g) plant-based ground beef, such as Impossible or Beyond

1 cup (35 g) fresh parsley leaves

½ medium white onion, diced

2 teaspoons minced fresh ginger

2 teaspoons minced garlic

1 teaspoon chili powder

1 teaspoon ground coriander

1 teaspoon ground cumin

¾ teaspoon ground black pepper

2 teaspoons unsalted plant-based butter, such as Earth Balance, at room temperature

½ cup (30 g) bread crumbs

Salt

FOR SERVING:

Pita bread, lettuce, cucumber, tomatoes, Kebab Shop Chili Sauce (page 227), Creamy Cashew-Based Tzatziki (page 226), steamed white basmati rice

EQUIPMENT:

Wooden skewers (see Note)

In a large bowl, add the beef, parsley, onion, ginger, garlic, chili powder, coriander, cumin, pepper, butter, bread crumbs, and salt and mix until well combined. Freeze the mixture for about 30 minutes (this will help the kebabs hold their shape).

Take the mixture out of the freezer and shape it into kebabs – tubes around 4 inches (10 cm) long and 1 inch (2.5 cm) thick – and skewer them. Alternatively, you can skip the skewers and shape the mixture into patties.

Preheat a grill to medium heat.

Place the kebabs on the grill and cook 6 to 8 minutes, until they are well browned and heated through, turning occasionally to ensure even cooking.

Serve them in pita bread with lettuce, cucumber, tomatoes, chili sauce, and tzatziki, or simply with basmati rice.

NOTE

SOAK FIRST: To prevent wooden skewers from catching fire while grilling, soak them in cool water for at least 30 minutes before loading them up.

Edgar's Vegan Goulash

SERVES 6

My family is full of exceptional cooks, and impressing them isn't an easy feat. This culinary gem comes from my father-in-law Edgar, affectionately known as Opa—the maestro of warmth and joy during our family's Christmas gatherings in Vienna, Austria.

On my wedding day in Vienna, Edgar decided to whip up this goulash, uncertain it would meet my family's expectations. We had a whole bunch of Jamaicans fly over for the big day, and they are picky eaters! Little did he know that it would quickly become a beloved favorite, making its way into our London kitchen.

The secret to the magic? Well, this goulash is actually reminiscent of curry goat and Jamaican pepper steak, creating an unexpected link between Austria and Jamaica. It goes to show you that food truly knows no boundaries—it's a universal language that brings us all together.

And that's exactly what it did in Opa's kitchen. Amid our blend of imperfect German and English—his native tongue and my own—we found a unique connection through food.

Opa's goulash has now become a cherished tradition, evolving gracefully to include vegan sausages and hearty potatoes, all served with hot, crusty bread. It's a dish that not only fills our bellies but also warms our hearts with memories of family and togetherness.

- 2 tablespoons neutral oil
- 5 large yellow onions, finely diced
- 2 cloves garlic, finely chopped
- 3 tablespoons Hungarian paprika or sweet paprika
- ¼ cup (60 ml) tomato paste
- 1 teaspoon marjoram
- 2 teaspoons caraway seeds
- ¾ teaspoon coriander seeds
- 8 cups (2 L) hot water
- ½ teaspoon fine salt
- ½ teaspoon ground black pepper
- 2 teaspoons soy sauce or tamari
- 2 bay leaves
- 1 cube vegan bouillon, crumbled
- 10 large, starchy potatoes, such as russet or yellow potatoes, peeled and cut into ¾-inch (2 cm) cubes
- Slices of dark bread, dinner rolls, or slices of baguette, for serving
- Sauerkraut, for serving (optional)

In a large pot, heat the oil over high heat. Add the onions and sauté for 5 minutes, stirring constantly. Reduce the heat to medium and continue cooking the onions, stirring often, for about 13 minutes or until translucent. Then add the garlic and cook for an additional 2 minutes, or until the onions are soft and golden brown.

Add the paprika, tomato paste, marjoram, caraway seeds, and coriander seeds. Stir for a few seconds.

Add the water, salt, pepper, soy sauce, bay leaves, and bouillon to the pot. Lower the heat to medium-low and simmer, uncovered, for 1 hour, stirring occasionally.

Add the potatoes and cook for an additional 30 minutes, or until the potatoes are soft. Fish out 10 pieces of potato and put them in a small bowl. Thoroughly mash them with a fork.

Add a ladle of the goulash liquid to the mashed potatoes, and stir to get a smooth paste. Transfer the mashed potato mixture back to the pot, stir, and cook for a couple more minutes. The sauce should thicken.

Serve the goulash with bread and sauerkraut, if desired. Store in an airtight container in the fridge for up to 3 days. If you reheat the goulash, the consistency will be thicker. It often tastes even better the next day.

PENSKE
PENSKE
Truck Rental

SNACK TIME IN MAURITIUS AND JAMAICA:

A STREET FOOD ADVENTURE

On the enchanting islands of Mauritius and Jamaica, the streets are where the culinary magic truly happens!

In Mauritius, you can find a huge array of vegetarian street food options—from fresh fruit to indulgent fried snacks—not only at huts on the side of the road but also at the many bustling open-air markets. At the Grand Baie Bazaar are street foods from all of Mauritius's cultures—Creole, African, Indian, and Chinese. But if you're specifically looking for Indo-Mauritian street food with Chinese-influences, head to the Flacq Market. It's the biggest open-air market on the island, and the most colorful. There, you'll not only end up with lots of great food, but you'll also be tempted to buy beautiful saris, fabrics, and dried tea leaves.

If you're looking for Mauritian fried delicacies like gâteau piment or gâteau arouille, check out the street-side stands all over the island early in the morning. They'll be frying up huge, fresh batches in massive woks. Just be careful, because you'll always think you'll stop at one but will end up ordering at least three servings.

In Jamaica, meanwhile, wander through the bustling streets and savor the mouthwatering scents of barbecue, the island's famous jerk seasoning, and tropical fruit. Reggae beats are playing, vendors are smiling, and colorful stalls are packed with delicious goodies like flaky beef patties, jerk corn on the cob, and fresh coconut water.

In this chapter, I'll teach you how to make some of those treats, which are among my favorite dishes from my love affair with Mauritian and Jamaican food.

Crispy Onion Bhajis

MAKES 30 FRITTERS

First up, bhajis are the undisputed kings of addictive street food. When I'm in Mauritius, there's an unwritten rule: we must make a pit stop for these irresistibly crunchy fritters made of battered, finely sliced onions. The craving hits you as soon as you step off the plane, and the only way to satisfy it is to pull over at the first stand you see and indulge in the pure delight of dipping them in your favorite sauce—it's hard to pick, but I'd recommend a cilantro chutney (page 220). This welcome-home treat sets the tone for all the flavorful adventures that await in Mauritius.

1 cup (90 g) chickpea flour

¼ cup (40 g) rice flour

1 teaspoon cumin seeds

½ teaspoon ground turmeric

½ teaspoon chili powder (adjust depending on your spice preference)

Salt

4 medium onions, sliced (I recommend using 2 red and 2 white or yellow)

Neutral oil, for frying

Satini Cotomili (Cilantro Chutney; page 220) or your preferred sweet chili sauce

In a large bowl, combine the chickpea flour, rice flour, cumin seeds, turmeric, chili powder, and salt to taste.

Add the onions and mix until they are well coated with the flour mixture.

Slowly incorporate ¾ cup (180 ml) water into the onion mixture while stirring continuously to form a thick batter. Let it rest for 30 minutes.

In a large frying pan over medium heat, heat 3 inches (7.5 cm) of vegetable oil to 340°F (170°C).

With a small spoon, drop a dollop of batter into the hot oil, constantly stirring the oil to allow the bhaji to puff up. Repeat with more batter, but do not crowd the pan. Fry until the bhajis are golden brown and crisp.

Carefully remove the bhajis from the oil using a spider to a paper towel, allowing excess oil to drain. Immediately season them with salt. Repeat with the remaining batter.

Serve the bhajis hot with satini cotomili.

Gâteau Piment (Chile Cakes)

MAKES 40 TO 50 CAKES

Gâteau piment, or "chile cakes," are some of the most popular Mauritian street foods. Because they're quite spicy, you'll often find another stand nearby selling vanilla tea to help you wash them down. Their scent transports me to the kitchen of my Mauritian childhood, where Auntie Marie made countless batches, frying for hours with the windows open.

Now these fritters have become a favorite at my parties. Whip up this recipe and join in reliving the joy of shared laughter, the hum of the food processor, and the aromas of cumin and chiles. Let's create a new cherished memory, one crispy bite at a time.

These fritters are sometimes compared to falafel, except they are made primarily of yellow split peas and chiles, not chickpeas. Enjoy them on their own, on freshly baked bread with plant-based butter, and/or with one of my Mauritian condiments (see Vegan Island Pantry, page 217). The addition of baking soda helps keep these fritters perfectly crisp for as long as possible.

- 2½ cups (500 g) yellow split peas (dholl)
- 3 teaspoons salt
- 1 teaspoon baking soda
- 2 teaspoons cumin seeds
- 1 tablespoon chopped fresh green chile, such as Kashmiri, Guntur, Byadgi, Kanthari, or Bhut Jolokia
- 1 medium white onion, diced
- 3 scallions, chopped
- ¼ cup (10 g) chopped fresh cilantro
- Neutral oil, for frying

In a large bowl, soak the yellow split peas in water to cover for at least 5 hours or preferably overnight.

Drain and rinse the split peas with fresh water.

Using a food processor, pulse the yellow split peas to a slightly grainy and chunky texture (do not blend to a smooth paste). This is crucial for keeping the gâteau piment crispy during frying.

Transfer the blended split peas to a large mixing bowl. Add the salt, baking soda, cumin seeds, chile, white onion, scallions, and cilantro and mix well. Form the mixture into small balls about 1 inch (2.5 cm) in diameter.

In a deep pot over medium-high heat, heat 3 inches (7.5 cm) of oil to 350°F (175°C) when measured with a deep-fry thermometer (see Note). Working in batches of 15, fry the balls for 8 to 10 minutes, or until they turn golden brown.

Carefully remove the balls from the oil using a spider, allowing excess oil to drain. Place them on a paper towel to absorb any additional oil. Serve immediately.

NOTE

NOT GREASY: Ensure your cooking oil is adequately hot before frying to prevent the gâteau piment from absorbing excess oil. Use a deep-fry thermometer to help maintain the correct temperature.

Mauritian Gâteau Arouille (Taro Fritters)

MAKES 20 FRITTERS

At the lively bazaar in Port Louis, Mauritius, the irresistible fragrance of piping-hot taro fritters wafts through the air in the mornings. This culinary gem comes from the vibrant Chinese community of Mauritius, and it has transcended borders, winning hearts far and wide. Taro is a starchy, earthy root vegetable that is delicious but does require some care when handling (see Note).

Sweet, salty, and gingery, these fritters have a crispy shell surrounding a soft and chewy center. The experience of eating them is not too different from enjoying a freshly fried donut, but they are so much easier to make. Re-creating these delights at home on a weekend morning is the perfect accompaniment to a leisurely tea-drinking session. As we say in the comforting melody of the Creole language, "weekend bien koumenser" ("the weekend has truly begun") when you have one of these fritters. They go perfectly with my Satini Cotomili (Cilantro Chutney; page 220).

4 slices white bread

2 pounds (910 g) taro (see Note)

1 (1-inch/2.5 cm) piece fresh ginger, peeled and minced

2 tablespoons sugar

1 teaspoon salt

2 tablespoons cornstarch

Neutral oil, for frying

In a medium bowl, cover the bread slices with water. Let the bread soak for 2 minutes, then drain. Squeeze any extra water from the bread and set aside.

Into a large bowl, grate the taro. Add the soaked bread, ginger, sugar, salt, and cornstarch. Mix everything by hand until well combined, forming a sticky, pliable mixture.

Form the mixture into about 20 balls, each approximately 1 inch (2.5 cm) in diameter.

In a deep pot over medium-high heat, heat 3 inches (7.5 cm) of oil to 350°F (175°C) when measured with a deep-fry thermometer. Once the oil is hot enough, gently place the taro balls into the oil. Working in batches of 10, fry for 7 to 8 minutes or until golden brown.

Carefully remove the taro fritters from the oil using a spider, allowing excess oil to drain. Place them on a paper towel to absorb any additional oil and let them cool before serving.

NOTE

TARO SAFETY: Handling taro can lead to skin irritation, particularly after peeling the outer layer. It's important to keep the peeled taro dry; avoid washing it, and instead use a damp paper towel to wipe away any dirt. Consider wearing rubber gloves for protection and exercise caution during preparation.

Jamaican Vegan Beef Puffs

MAKES 6 PUFFS

Let's keep it real—I don't always have the time or patience to make a flaky pastry from scratch. That's why, in this cheeky twist on the classic Jamaican beef patty I grew up with, I opt for store-bought puff pastry.

Jamaican beef patties hold a special spot in Caribbean culinary culture, often enjoyed as a savory snack or meal on the go by locals and visitors alike. The buttery, flaky pastry encases a flavorful filling of spiced ground beef, onions, peppers, and sometimes carrots, creating a delicious handheld treat. As long as the filling is on point, we're in for a tasty ride!

- 2 pounds (910 g) plant-based ground beef, such as Impossible or Beyond
- ½ teaspoon ground black pepper
- 1 teaspoon ground allspice
- 2 tablespoons neutral oil
- 1 cup (125 g) diced red onion
- 2 teaspoons minced garlic
- 1 tablespoon fresh or dried thyme leaves
- Salt
- Splash of tamari or soy sauce
- ½ cup (35 g) Jamaican curry powder
- ¼ cup (60 ml) tomato paste
- All-purpose flour
- 1 sheet store-bought puff pastry, such as Pepperidge Farm
- Refined coconut oil, for brushing pastry
- Scotch Bonnet Mango Hot Sauce (page 225), for serving

In a large bowl, combine the beef with the pepper and allspice and mix well. Set aside.

In a frying pan over medium heat, heat the oil. Add the onion and sauté for 6 to 7 minutes, until translucent. Add the garlic and thyme and sauté for another minute. Season with salt to taste.

Add the beef to the pan, breaking up any clumps. Add the tamari, curry powder, tomato paste, and 2 cups (480 ml) water. Bring the mixture to a boil, then reduce the heat and let it simmer until most of the liquid has evaporated. Remove from the heat and let the filling cool completely.

Preheat the oven to 400°F (205°C). Line a baking sheet with parchment paper.

Flour your work surface. Cut the puff pastry into 5-inch (12 cm) circles.

Add 2 tablespoons of the cooled filling to the center of each piece of pastry. Moisten the edges of the pastry with water. Fold the pastry in half and press the edges together to seal. With a fork, crimp the edges together. Place the puffs on the prepared baking sheet and brush with the coconut oil.

Bake the beef puffs for 15 to 20 minutes, until golden brown. If you want a rich, dark brown, let them bake for 2 to 3 minutes more.

Cool the puffs on wire racks and serve with hot sauce.

Grilled Jerk Corn on the Cob

SERVES 6

There's something truly special about the foods you discover on the side of the road in Jamaica, especially in jerk huts. One staple that captures the essence of the island's street-food experience is the grilled corn on the cob.

Freshly picked corn, just shucked and blanched, meets the sizzling heat of a grill, filling the air with the smoky aroma of jerk seasoning. As a kid, I loved to indulge in these delectable treats from roadside huts. The sheer joy of sinking my teeth into the smoky goodness—so eagerly that the corn would get stuck in my teeth—left a lasting impression.

My rendition keeps it simple but packs a punch with a homemade jerk dry rub. So gather around your grill pan, let the jerk butter mixture melt into every crevice of the corn, and relish the nostalgia of Jamaican street food right at your table. It's perfect for summer gatherings.

And yes—you might find yourself smiling with a bit of corn stuck in your teeth, just like the good old days!

6 ears fresh sweet corn, shucked

½ cup (115 g) unsalted plant-based butter, such as Earth Balance, at room temperature

2 tablespoons Jerk Dry Rub Seasoning (page 229), plus more as needed and for garnish

Fill a large pot halfway with water and bring it to a simmer over high heat.

Add the corn to the pot and cook for about 4 minutes, until slightly tender when pierced with a fork. Remove the corn from the pot and stack on a platter.

Preheat a grill pan to medium-high.

In a small bowl, combine the butter and the jerk dry rub. Adjust the amount of dry rub according to your spice preference.

Once the grill pan is hot, add half of the butter and jerk dry rub mixture to the pan.

Arrange the corn on the grill pan. Grill for about 5 minutes, turning often to slightly char all sides and brushing with the remaining jerk butter mixture.

Transfer the grilled corn to a serving platter. Sprinkle extra jerk dry rub over the corn for an additional burst of flavor if you'd like. Serve immediately.

Roasted and Fried Breadfruit Wedges

SERVES 4 TO 6

Breadfruit is a tropical fruit that belongs to the mulberry and jackfruit family. It's known for its starchy texture and creamy, mild flavor, somewhat like potatoes.

In Jamaica, breadfruit is a popular food and is prepared in different ways, including by roasting it until the skin is charred. The flesh is then scooped out and served with dishes like ackee and saltfish, curry, or jerk chicken. It can also be boiled and mashed like potatoes or fried into crispy slices, which are commonly eaten with fish dishes or as a snack. You can find it here in the US in Caribbean and Asian markets.

For this side dish, we'll roast and fry it to crispy perfection! Serve this side with my Ackee and "No Saltfish" (page 42) or simply enjoy the crispy goodness on its own. Experiment with different seasonings or dipping sauces.

1 breadfruit, about 64 ounces (1.8 kg) (see Notes)

1 teaspoon plus 2 tablespoons unrefined coconut oil

½ teaspoon salt, plus more as needed

Preheat the oven to 375°F (190°C).

Rinse the breadfruit and dry it well. Use a paring knife to carve out the stem and make a small "x" on the opposite end. Lightly rub 1 teaspoon of the oil all over the skin.

Place the prepared breadfruit directly on the oven rack. Roast for 60 to 90 minutes, until the skin turns dark brown and both ends of the fruit are visibly steaming.

Carefully remove the breadfruit from the oven and allow it to cool. Peel off the skin, cut it in half lengthwise, and scoop out the core. Slice each half into ½-inch-thick (12 mm) wedges (see Notes).

In a large skillet over medium-high heat, heat the remaining 2 tablespoons oil. Season the breadfruit wedges with salt, then, working in batches, place them in the skillet cut side down. Fry the wedges, flipping once, until they become crispy and golden brown – approximately 4 to 5 minutes per side. Remove the fried breadfruit wedges from the skillet and drain them on a paper towel–lined plate. Repeat with the remaining wedges.

Season with additional salt, if desired, before serving.

NOTES

TIPS ON BUYING BREADFRUIT:

Appearance: Look for breadfruit that is free from blemishes, bruises, or cuts on the skin. The skin should be firm and without any soft spots.

Weight: Pick up the breadfruit and assess its weight. A heavier breadfruit typically indicates juiciness and maturity.

Texture: Gently press the breadfruit with your fingers. Ripe breadfruit will yield slightly to pressure without being too soft, while unripe breadfruit will feel firm and dense.

Ripe vs. Unripe: Breadfruit can be eaten both when ripe and unripe. Ripe breadfruit will have a softer texture and a yellowish-green color, with a slightly sweet aroma. Unripe breadfruit is firmer and has a green color and is often used for cooking, as it's less sweet and starchier. For this recipe, either ripe or unripe will work just fine.

STORING BREADFRUIT: You can freeze the sliced breadfruit. To use later, simply defrost, pat dry, and follow the frying instructions.

Fried Bakes

SERVES 4

Fried bakes, also known as "festivals" or "johnnycakes," are a popular type of bread in Caribbean and West Indian cuisine, characterized by their crispy exteriors and soft, fluffy interiors. Fried bakes are made from a dough consisting of flour, sugar, salt, baking powder, butter, and water. They are shaped into small balls or elongated shapes and fried until golden brown.

Fried bakes are a favorite street food in Jamaica and are often served alongside savory dishes like jerk chicken or fish. They are also enjoyed as a snack or side dish at home and are a staple in many Caribbean households.

Whenever I'm whipping up my Green Banana Rundown (page 84) and the kitchen's buzzing with island vibes, I can't resist the lure of making some golden fried bakes to go along with it. Rundown and bakes are the dynamic duo of my Caribbean kitchen.

Now, I have a confession: sometimes, I let the aroma of the fresh fried bakes take over, and I decide to treat myself. In a moment of sheer indulgence, I sneak a fried bake from the pan and eat it while it's still sizzling hot—with a generous dash of cinnamon sugar, of course. I don't even wait for the whole batch to finish! It's my little rebellion, and every bite is cinnamon-infused bliss.

These crispy, fluffy delights are incredibly versatile. Try adding raisins, dried currants, or little pieces of apple to the dough before frying. Make them your own!

- ⅓ cup (80 ml) lukewarm water
- 1 tablespoon sugar
- 1 tablespoon instant yeast
- 4 cups (500 g) all-purpose flour, plus more for dusting
- 2 tablespoons unsalted plant-based butter, such as Earth Balance, at room temperature
- ¼ cup (50 g) coconut brown sugar
- 1¼ tablespoons baking powder
- 1 teaspoon salt
- ½ teaspoon ground nutmeg
- ½ teaspoon ground cinnamon
- 2 cups (480 ml) neutral oil, for frying

In a small bowl, combine the water with the sugar and the yeast. Allow the mixture to sit for 5 minutes, until foamy.

To a large bowl, add the flour and butter. Incorporate the butter well using your fingertips.

Add the sugar, baking powder, salt, nutmeg, and cinnamon and mix well to combine. Stir in the proofed yeast and water.

Knead the mixture for about 5 minutes, until a smooth dough ball is formed. Divide the dough into 12 balls about 2 inches (5 cm) in diameter.

Line a baking sheet with parchment paper, dust it with a bit of flour, and set the dough balls on it. Cover the sheet with a dish towel and let the yeast do its magic for around 20 minutes at room temperature; the dough balls will double in size.

In a large frying pan over medium heat, heat the oil. Once the oil is hot, place the dough balls into the oil in batches of about 4 at a time, as they will expand in the oil. They should sizzle immediately; if not, increase the temperature of the oil. Fry around 7 minutes on each side, until golden brown.

Remove the bakes from the oil with a spider and place them in a small foil pan lined with a paper towel to drain any excess oil.

NOTES

Before frying, the dough for fried bakes has a smooth, elastic texture. It's slightly sticky but manageable, similar to bread dough. The dough is elastic but not overly stiff, allowing it to be formed into flat discs easily. When you press it between your fingers, it should retain its shape without sticking excessively to your hands.

SIDE DISHES

These side dishes showcase the best vegetables and legumes that Jamaica and Mauritius have to offer! But it would be doing them a disservice simply to view them as sides; you could be content eating a bowl of most of these dishes on their own, as I often did as a kid.

Gone are the days of boiled, bland potatoes and soggy green beans—each of these recipes is elevated with spices, herbs, and island flair. Even if you're not usually a fan of cabbage or lentils, you may find a new way of approaching these ingredients that will change your mind forever.

I also hope that this section shows you the culinary potential of some underestimated ingredients: you can turn a humble can of kidney beans into a delicious, satisfying meal. These recipes prove that vegan food doesn't deserve its reputation of being expensive and bland. Vegetables (whether from your garden, the produce section at your local supermarket, or a can) can be affordable, delicious, and easy to prepare!

Rougaille Sauce (Tomato Sauce)

MAKES 6 CUPS (1.4 L)

In this cookbook, you'll frequently encounter rougaille, the cornerstone of many Mauritian dishes. Rougaille is a beloved Mauritian sauce with a rich tomato base and a harmonious blend of flavors from onions, garlic, ginger, thyme, cilantro, and curry leaves. Think of it as the Mauritian equivalent of Italian marinara sauce, serving as a foundational element for a variety of recipes.

Whether you prefer to call it rougaille, tomato sauce, red sauce, or spicy Creole sauce, for many Mauritians, this dish signifies the warmth of home-cooked comfort. Every Mauritian family has its own version. With rougaille as the foundation, Mauritius has woven a vibrant tapestry of flavors that reflects its diverse culinary influences. In the days leading up to Mauritius's independence in 1968, when luxuries were scarce, rougaille emerged as a cherished classic in daily meals. Now, rougaille is deeply ingrained in Creole Mauritian cuisine and has become a kitchen essential across the island.

You can serve it as a side with dishes like Mauritian Lentil Crepes (page 92), Bouillon Cresson (Watercress Broth; page 98), and No Shrimp Curry (page 107). Make it a meal by simply adding plain white basmati rice or a protein. To this base sauce you can add any plant-based meat, seafood, eggs, or tofu, catering to all dietary preferences—there's a rougaille for everyone! I love to add vegan salted fish and dried shrimp, which add a salty punch to the sauce.

2 tablespoons neutral oil

1 large white onion, diced

5 sprigs thyme

2 tablespoons minced fresh ginger

2 tablespoons minced garlic

6 fresh curry leaves

Salt

2¼ cups (400 g) chopped fresh ripe tomatoes

Chopped fresh cilantro

3 green chiles, sliced lengthwise

In a large saucepan over medium-high heat, heat the oil. When the oil is hot, add the onion, thyme, ginger, garlic, and curry leaves. Sauté for 2 minutes, then add salt to taste and cook until the onion softens, about 5 minutes more.

Add the tomatoes and ½ cup (120 ml) water. Bring to a simmer and then turn the heat to low, cover, and simmer for 15 minutes.

Add the cilantro and green chiles and simmer for another 5 minutes to let the flavors infuse. When the tomatoes have softened and broken down and the sauce has thickened, remove the thyme sprigs and serve.

Store in an airtight container in the fridge for up to 3 days or freeze for up to 1 month.

Rougaille Pistache (Mauritian Peanut Sauce)

SERVES 4

My mum and Uncle Bluey often dive into nostalgic tales of their younger days, especially from times that were financially tight when they moved to London from Mauritius in the seventies. In those moments, all it took to create something special was a jar of crunchy peanut butter, basic rougaille ingredients, and a loaf of bread—and just like that, they had a satisfying and comforting meal. The magic wasn't in elaborate recipes or gourmet ingredients, but in the resourcefulness and creativity that turned humble components into something truly special.

This spicy peanut sauce is a symbol of resilience and a reminder that simple pleasures make life rich in their own way. My family serves this rougaille with a warm, crusty baguette straight out of the oven, simply breaking off pieces of bread and dipping them straight into the sauce!

- 2 tablespoons neutral oil
- 1 large white onion, diced
- 1 bunch thyme sprigs
- 1 tablespoon grated fresh ginger
- 1 tablespoon store-bought garlic paste
- 6 fresh curry leaves
- 1 teaspoon salt, or more as needed
- 2¼ cups (400 g) chopped ripe tomatoes
- 6 tablespoons (90 ml) crunchy peanut butter (see Note)
- Sliced red and green chiles, for garnish

In a large saucepan over medium heat, heat the oil. When the oil is hot, add the onion, thyme, grated ginger, garlic paste, and curry leaves. Sauté for 2 minutes, then add the salt and cook until the onion is soft, about 5 minutes.

Add the tomatoes and ½ cup (120 ml) water. Bring to a simmer and then turn the heat to low, cover, and simmer for 15 minutes.

Add the peanut butter and mix until fully combined. The sauce will become thick, so add a little water if you prefer a thinner consistency. Season with salt to taste and take off the heat.

Remove the thyme sprigs, garnish with chiles, and you are ready to serve.

NOTE

GO NUTS: You can also use smooth peanut butter instead of crunchy, but I personally prefer a bit more texture.

Vegetable Achard (Pickled Vegetables)

MAKES 2 (16-OUNCE/480 ML) MASON JARS

Hey, pickle enthusiasts! Meet vegetable achard, a Mauritian sensation. Think chopped veggies in a zesty mix of mustard seeds, turmeric, ginger, and a hint of chile, all soaked in vinegar. It's a flavor bomb! Pair the pickles with rice or Effortless Homemade Chapatis (Indian Flatbread; page 153)—the tangy kick and spiciness will turn every bite into a taste extravaganza. Enjoy these pickles in baguettes, rotis, wraps, or alone as a tasty snack.

1 teaspoon salt

3 carrots, julienned or coarsely grated

½ white cabbage, thinly sliced

¼ cup (60 ml) neutral oil, plus more as needed

2 cloves garlic, crushed

2 teaspoons mustard seeds, crushed

1 teaspoon turmeric

6 long green chiles, halved lengthwise

1 sweet red pepper, thinly sliced

2 large white or yellow onions, sliced

2 tablespoons distilled white vinegar

EQUIPMENT:

2 (16-ounce/480 ml) Mason jars

Wash two Mason jars with soap and hot water. Bring a large pot filled with water to a boil, add the salt, then remove from the heat. Immediately drop the carrots and cabbage in the water and blanch for 2 minutes. Remove the vegetables from the water quickly and drain.

On a tray lined with parchment paper, spread out the blanched vegetables and let them dry at room temperature for 3 to 4 hours.

In a wok over high heat, heat the oil until very hot, then remove from the heat. Add the garlic, mustard seeds, turmeric, green chiles, sweet red pepper, and onions. Then add the blanched and dried vegetables and the vinegar and stir well to combine.

Let the vegetables cool completely, then pack them tightly into the Mason jars. Top the vegetables with additional oil to fill any empty space. Allow the vegetables to pickle for 2 days before eating.

Store the jars in the fridge for up to 3 months.

Fricasser Lentilles Noires (Mauritian Black Lentil Soup)

SERVES 2

Lentils are the unsung heroes of my pantry! They're an absolute staple in my household, and black lentils hold a special place in my heart. Coming home from school to a bowl of black lentil soup on a gray, drizzly day in East London was everything. We threw every spice imaginable into that pot, creating a warm and comforting masterpiece. Once you make lentil soup this way, you will never go back. Serve with aromatic basmati rice and Lisou Touffé (Mauritian Sautéed Cabbage; page 140) or enjoy the soup's rich flavors on their own.

- 1 cup (190 g) black lentils
- 1 teaspoon salt, plus more as needed
- 2 small carrots, diced
- 1 red tomato, diced
- 2 tablespoons refined coconut oil
- 5 or 6 fresh curry leaves
- 3 sprigs thyme
- 1 or 2 dried chile peppers
- 1 teaspoon grated fresh ginger
- 1 teaspoon store-bought garlic paste
- Pinch of cumin seeds
- 2 tablespoons finely chopped scallion
- Piment Crazée (Mauritian Chile Garlic Paste; page 221)

Rinse the black lentils with cold water and drain. To a medium pot, add the lentils, salt, and 3 cups (720 ml) water. Bring to a boil over medium-high heat, then reduce the heat to maintain a simmer. Simmer the lentils for 15 minutes, then taste them to check for doneness. They should be tender to the bite. Add the carrots and tomato and simmer for 5 minutes before turning off the heat so that they cook and soften but still retain some bite. Season with salt to taste. If the soup is too thick, add up to ½ cup (120 ml) water to reach your desired consistency. Set aside, covered, to keep warm.

Meanwhile, in a small cast-iron pan over medium heat, heat the oil to prepare for tempering. When the oil is hot, add the curry leaves, thyme, dried chiles, grated ginger, garlic paste, and cumin seeds. Allow the spices to become fragrant and then sizzle and sputter, stirring for about 30 seconds, then turn off the heat. Remove the thyme sprigs.

Stir the tempered oil into the lentils and garnish with scallion and piment crazée, and serve.

Lisou Touffé (Mauritian Sautéed Cabbage)

SERVES 4

Lisou touffé is a traditional dish from Mauritius consisting of thinly sliced cabbage and potatoes that are first sautéed and then braised with a combination of spices and aromatics. This simple but flavorful preparation holds a special place in my heart—it's my grand-mère's signature dish. Eating it brings back childhood memories of returning home after church on a Saturday afternoon, eagerly anticipating the aroma that filled the kitchen.

Grand-mère would pair it with white rice and Rougaille Saucisse (Sausages in Tomato Sauce; page 80). But what made it truly special was our little game: with a mischievous twinkle in her eye, she'd feed me a spoonful and say, "One for you and one for me." These moments of love and connection made lisou touffé a cherished tradition in our family.

- 2 tablespoons neutral oil
- 1 teaspoon black mustard seeds
- 1 medium red onion, sliced
- 3 or 4 dried red chiles, broken in half
- 1 teaspoon cumin seeds
- 5 fresh curry leaves
- 4 sprigs thyme
- 1 teaspoon minced fresh ginger
- 2 cloves garlic, minced
- 1 medium green cabbage, thinly sliced
- 2 medium Yukon Gold potatoes, peeled and cubed
- 1 small tomato, chopped
- 1 teaspoon salt
- Steamed white basmati rice, for serving
- Your preferred chutney (see pages 220, 222–224)

In a cast-iron pan over medium heat, heat the oil to prepare for tempering. When the oil is hot, add one mustard seed: when it sizzles, the oil is ready. Add the remaining mustard seeds and let them start to pop, then add the onion, chiles, cumin seeds, and curry leaves and sauté for 2 to 3 minutes.

Add the thyme, ginger, and garlic and cook for 1 minute. Add the cabbage, potatoes, tomato, salt, and 2 cups (480 ml) water. Cover and cook until the potatoes are soft, about 30 minutes.

Remove the thyme sprigs and serve with rice and, as always, one of the chutneys in my condiments section.

Callaloo Sauté

SERVES 4

This Jamaican callaloo sauté, a quick and flavorful side dish, has always been a favorite. If you're familiar with Southern cuisine, think of the leafy green callaloo as the Caribbean version of collard greens or Swiss chard—delicious, nutritious, and a staple in Jamaican soups, stews, and sides.

Fresh callaloo is hard to find, so I generally use canned. Canned callaloo is typically sold in a brine to preserve its freshness. When using canned callaloo, it's important to drain and rinse the leaves before cooking to remove excess brine.

Pair it with Ackee and "No Saltfish" (page 42) or enjoy it alongside Roasted and Fried Breadfruit Wedges (page 126).

The combination of vibrant vegetables, aromatic herbs, and Scotch bonnet spice offers a true taste of the Caribbean in one quick and easy recipe!

- 2 tablespoons olive oil
- 1 medium yellow onion, chopped
- 2 scallions, chopped, plus more for optional garnish
- 1 Scotch bonnet pepper, chopped
- 2 cloves garlic, minced
- 1 (19-ounce/540 g) can callaloo, drained and rinsed
- 2 Roma tomatoes, chopped
- 1 teaspoon fresh thyme leaves, plus more for optional garnish
- ¼ teaspoon ground black pepper
- 2 tablespoons liquid aminos (optional)

In a large skillet over medium heat, heat the olive oil. Add the yellow onion, scallions, Scotch bonnet pepper, and garlic and sauté for 4 to 6 minutes, or until the onions soften.

Add the callaloo, tomatoes, thyme leaves, and black pepper. For a smoky flavor, consider adding a splash of liquid aminos. Stir the ingredients together to combine, and cook until the mixture is heated through, approximately 5 minutes, allowing the flavors to meld together.

Transfer to a serving dish and garnish with additional thyme leaves or scallions, if desired.

Jamaican Cabbage and Bacon

SERVES 4

The combination of cabbage and bacon in Jamaican cuisine is influenced by both African and European culinary traditions. Cabbage, being a versatile and readily available vegetable, is used in various dishes across the Caribbean. Bacon, on the other hand, was introduced to Jamaica during the colonial period by European settlers, particularly the British. Over time, this dish has become a popular comfort food in Jamaican households and is enjoyed as a flavorful side dish or main course.

Bacon adds a savory and smoky flavor to the dish, while cabbage provides a sweet and slightly crunchy element. Jamaican spices and aromatics, such as thyme, garlic, onions, and Jamaican allspice (pimento), add a distinct Caribbean flair.

My grandma Bernice, a culinary magician in her own right, used to whip up this humble yet heartwarming meal for us grandchildren. Paired with a side of rice, it was all we needed to feel content. My granddad Ferdinand, ever the green thumb, contributed by plucking fresh thyme straight from the garden and tossing it into the pan. The aroma of sizzling bacon would mingle with the sound of sautéing veggies and the earthy fragrance of thyme.

Even today, when I make this recipe, the kitchen becomes a portal to the past, bringing back the warmth of family and the delicious simplicity of Grandma's cooking. And now with Thrilling Foods' plant-based bacon, everything is possible!

- 1 (8-ounce/225 g) pack plant-based bacon strips, such as Thrilling Foods
- 3 tablespoons neutral oil
- 1 medium white onion, chopped
- 2 cloves garlic, finely chopped
- Leaves from 4 thyme sprigs
- ¼ Scotch bonnet pepper, seeds removed and finely chopped (optional)
- 1 Roma tomato, diced
- 1 medium white cabbage (about 1½ pounds/710 g), thinly sliced
- 1 green or red bell pepper, chopped
- 2 carrots, peeled and julienned
- 2½ teaspoons salt, plus more if needed
- ½ teaspoon ground black pepper

Slice the bacon horizontally into lardons about ¼ inch (6 mm) wide.

In a large cast-iron pan over medium-high heat, heat the oil. Add the bacon strips and fry until crispy. Place the bacon pieces on paper towels to absorb any excess oil and set aside.

Keeping the pan on the heat, in the same oil you used for the bacon, sauté the onion until translucent, 5 to 6 minutes.

Add the garlic, thyme, and Scotch bonnet pepper, if using, and sauté for about 2 minutes, until everything starts to soften and is fragrant.

Add the tomato and sauté for 1 minute, or until it starts to soften. Stir in the cabbage. Cover and let the mixture steam for 10 minutes.

Stir in the bell pepper and carrots, then add the salt and black pepper. Cover and steam for another 10 minutes, or until the cabbage is tender.

Take the dish off the heat and add the crispy bacon just before serving.

Mauritian Cucumber Salad

SERVES 4

Savor the simplicity of this salad, the perfect side dish for your spicy curries, like Green Curry with Tofu Fish, Eggplant, and Rice Cakes (page 75). It brings together the crispness of cucumber and the zing of lemon to offer a quick and easy balance to the heat in your favorite island dishes. A Mauritian staple, this refreshing dish is a taste of the tropics on your plate. Opt for extra-virgin olive oil instead of regular olive oil to bring this salad to the next level.

½ medium red onion, finely chopped

¼ bunch cilantro, finely chopped

2 cucumbers (preferably Lebanese or Persian), peeled, halved lengthwise, and sliced

1 fresh red chile, thinly sliced

1 teaspoon lemon juice

Extra virgin olive oil

Salt and ground black pepper

In a salad bowl, combine the onion, cilantro, cucumbers, chile, and lemon juice. Mix well.

Drizzle with olive oil until all the vegetables are coated.

Season with salt and pepper to taste and serve immediately. (If preparing in advance, add the salt just before serving to keep the salad fresh, as salt will draw liquid out. I would not recommend storing this salad.)

Haricots Rouges (Spiced Red Kidney Beans) and Rice

SERVES 4 TO 6

Beans and rice are a universally loved combination, but the Mauritian spices make this version of the classic dish particularly aromatic, and the coconut cream adds richness. This simple, comforting dish is a delicious and satisfying addition to any meal, perfect for both busy days and leisurely occasions!

- 2 tablespoons olive oil
- 1 large white onion, diced
- 1 tablespoon minced garlic
- 2 teaspoons minced ginger
- 1 teaspoon cumin seeds
- 1 teaspoon fresh thyme leaves
- 4 fresh curry leaves
- 1 teaspoon garam masala
- ¼ cup (60 ml) tomato puree
- ½ cup (120 ml) canned coconut cream
- 4 (15-ounce/425 g) cans kidney beans, undrained
- Salt
- Thyme sprigs, for garnish
- Steamed white basmati rice, for serving

In a large saucepan over medium-low heat, heat the olive oil. Add the onion, garlic, ginger, and cumin seeds and sauté until softened, 6 to 7 minutes.

Add the thyme leaves, curry leaves, and garam masala, then pour in the tomato puree, 1 cup (240 ml) water, and the coconut cream. Increase the heat to medium and bring to a simmer.

Stir in the beans with their liquid, then season with salt to taste.

Reduce the heat to low and let the mixture simmer for 30 minutes, stirring occasionally. If the sauce thickens too much, gradually add some hot water to achieve your desired consistency. Add more salt as needed.

Garnish with thyme sprigs and serve over rice.

Red
Stripe
Jamaican
LAGER BEER

Pilau Rice

SERVES 4

Pilau rice, also spelled *pilaf* or *pilaff*, is a fragrant and flavorful rice dish that originates from the Middle East but has variations and adaptations in many cultures worldwide, including Indian, Persian, Central Asian, and African cuisines. The dish typically consists of long-grain rice cooked with a blend of spices and aromatics.

In my kitchen, rice reigns supreme—it's the heart of all our meals. From the simplicity of plain basmati to the wholesome goodness of brown rice, the vibrant hue of yellow rice, or the earthy richness of wild rice, we're feasting on it daily!

One of our absolute favorites is this aromatic Pilau Rice. It pairs seamlessly with a variety of dishes, enhancing any meal with that perfect touch of fragrance from the cloves, cardamom, turmeric, and cinnamon.

1½ cups (270 g) white basmati rice

1 tablespoon neutral oil

2 whole cloves

2 green cardamom pods, bashed

1 (1½-inch/4 cm) piece cinnamon stick

1 teaspoon ground turmeric

Salt

Place the rice in a bowl and cover with water. Swirl the grains around, then drain the water. Repeat three more times, until the water runs clear. Allow the rice to drain completely.

In a medium pot over medium heat, heat the oil to prepare for tempering. When the oil is hot, add the cloves, cardamom pods, and cinnamon stick. Fry for 30 seconds or until aromatic. Immediately add the turmeric, followed by the rice. Add a pinch of salt and stir until all the rice grains are coated in the oil.

Increase the heat to high and add 1⅓ cups (315 ml) water, ensuring the water level sits just above the rice. Bring the water to a boil, uncovered, as quickly as possible.

Once boiling, cover the pot and transfer it to the smallest burner on your stove over the lowest heat. Cook for 20 minutes, then turn off the heat and let it sit, covered, for another 5 minutes. Resist the urge to open the lid during this time.

Uncover the pot and fluff up the rice grains with a fork. You can discard the whole spices before serving, if you prefer.

Fried Plantains

SERVES 2

A staple in every Jamaican household, fried plantains are both simple and essential. No matter how many you fry up, there never seems to be enough. Perhaps it's because I can't resist snacking on them while I'm busy frying a batch! These golden slices of deliciousness are a cherished part of our meals—a bit crispy on the outside, sweet and tender on the inside. Perfect for a tasty snack or a side dish.

I eat fried plantains with everything, and have since I was a kid. One of my favorite ways to serve them is in my Tropical Plantain and "Egg" Breakfast Sandwiches (page 66), adding a touch of Jamaican flair to my morning! You can also add a bit of spice, if you cook them with vegan spicy honey.

1 large ripe plantain

1 teaspoon plant-based hot honey, such as Mellody Spicy Habanero (optional)

2 tablespoons unrefined coconut oil

Peel the plantain and cut the fruit diagonally into slices about 1 inch (2.5 cm) thick. A big plantain should produce about 6 or 7 slices. If you want bold sweetness with a bit of a kick, drizzle 1 teaspoon of habanero honey over the plantains.

In a medium nonstick pan over medium heat, warm up the oil. Once the oil is good and hot, add the plantain slices. Cook until the edges get a nice brown color, about 2 minutes. Then, flip 'em over, starting with the first one you added to the pan. Repeat this flip-and-cook routine on both sides, cooking for about 2 minutes per side.

Take the golden, delicious plantains out of the pan and put them on a plate lined with a paper towel to cool and drain any excess oil.

Effortless Homemade Chapatis (Indian Flatbread)

SERVES 2

Welcome to the quick and delightful world of homemade chapatis! In under fifteen minutes, you'll be savoring warm, soft chapatis that rival any restaurant's offerings. All it takes is a handful of pantry staples and a dash of enthusiasm, and you're on your way to a delicious Indian flatbread right in your own kitchen. These flavorful chapatis never fail to hit the spot! Serve them hot with your favorite curries, such as No Shrimp Curry (page 107), dip them into your favorite condiments, or use them to make wraps.

- ⅔ cup (80 g) atta flour (see Notes), sifted, plus more for dusting
- ⅛ teaspoon salt
- ½ tablespoon unrefined coconut oil
- ⅓ cup (80 ml) boiling water
- All-purpose flour, for dusting

In a small bowl, combine the flour, salt, and oil. Pour in the boiling water and mix with a spatula until a rough dough forms.

Lightly flour your work surface. Knead the dough until it becomes soft and smooth, about 5 minutes. Divide the dough into 4 equal-sized round balls, about 1½ ounces (40 g) each.

Using a small rolling pin, roll each dough ball into a 6-inch (15 cm) round, or to your desired thickness. Dust with flour as needed to prevent sticking.

Heat a skillet over medium heat. Once hot, place a rolled-out chapati onto the pan. Cook for about 1 minute, or until lightly browned on one side, then flip and cook for another minute on the other side.

Place the cooked chapati on a plate and cover with a towel to keep warm. Repeat the cooking process with the remaining rolled-out chapatis and serve them immediately while warm or store for a later use (see Notes).

NOTES

SWAP OPTION: Atta flour is available in Indian grocery stores, but if you can't find it, use white whole wheat flour instead.

STORING YOUR CHAPATIS: Chapati dough can be stored in the fridge for a few days. Let it sit at room temperature for 30 minutes before rolling it out and cooking. After cooking, take a piece of foil and place one chapati on it. Then place another piece of foil on top of the chapati, followed by another chapati. Repeat until you have a stack. This makes it easy to remove individual chapatis without thawing the entire stack. Wrap the entire stack tightly in an additional layer of foil to prevent freezer burn. Place each stack in an individual freezer bag, squeeze out any air to prevent ice crystals from forming, and seal it tightly. The cooked chapatis can be stored in the fridge for up to 5 days, or in the freezer for up to 3 months. Reheat them in the microwave whenever needed.

Spicy Baked Okra Fries

SERVES 4

Okra fries are a beloved Indian Mauritian street food. As a child, I wasn't fond of okra, which is also known as "ladies' fingers" in Mauritius, mainly because my aunts always simmered them in curries, and I objected to the slimy texture. However, my perspective changed drastically when I encountered crispy and flavorful okra fries at the street market. It's fascinating how our tastes evolve over time, turning childhood dislikes into adult favorites. Nowadays, I absolutely adore okra prepared in any way, and my daughter shares the same enthusiasm.

If you're hesitant about okra because of its texture, these delicious okra fries might just change your mind and spark a newfound love for this versatile vegetable. Baked at a high temperature, they achieve the perfect crunch without any greasiness! They're not just a snack or appetizer; they're a delicious revelation in the world of okra dishes. Experiment with dipping sauces—my tangy Tamarind Sauce (page 219) takes these fries to a whole new level.

- 1 pound (455 g) fresh okra, washed and dried
- 2 tablespoons olive oil
- 1 teaspoon ground cumin
- 1 teaspoon paprika
- ½ teaspoon cayenne pepper (adjust to your spice level)
- ½ teaspoon garlic powder
- ½ teaspoon onion powder
- Salt and ground black pepper

Preheat the oven to 425°F (220°C). Lay some parchment paper on a baking sheet for convenient cleanup.

Trim the ends off the okra and slice them lengthwise into thin strips resembling fries. Give them a quick pat with a paper towel to get rid of excess moisture.

In a large bowl, combine the olive oil, cumin, paprika, cayenne, garlic powder, onion powder, salt, and black pepper. Stir well to create the spicy seasoning mix.

Toss the sliced okra in the seasoning mix until each piece has a good coating.

Spread the seasoned okra pieces in a single layer on the baking sheet. Give them some space so they can crisp up properly.

Bake the okra for 20 to 25 minutes, flipping the fries halfway through, until beautifully golden brown. Let the okra cool for a moment before diving in.

Margose Frire (Stir-Fried Bitter Gourd)

SERVES 4

Margose, the bitter gourd! I have loved this veggie, which is also known as karela or bitter melon, since I was a kid—stir-fried, curried, in soups, or cooked with vindaye spices (see page 87).

Bitter gourd has a distinctive flavor, a combination of bitterness, earthiness, subtle sweetness, and a hint of tanginess that adds a unique depth to dishes. The bitterness makes it an acquired taste for some, not too dissimilar to broccoli rabe or bitter lettuces like radicchio.

When cooked, bitter gourd softens while it retains its characteristic bitter flavor, which can be balanced with the addition of spice, acid, and fat—as I do in this stir-fry that I love to serve alongside steamed basmati rice. This dish is one of my favorite sides to pair with any dinner. Bitter gourd also offers many health benefits. It's been used medicinally for centuries and can balance digestion, boost the immune system, help manage diabetes, aid in weight loss, and even keep your eyes sharp. Plus, since it's packed with antioxidants, it's a secret to radiant beauty. Who knew bitter could be so sweet?

6 medium bitter gourds, about 20 ounces (600 g)

2 tablespoons salt

2 tablespoons neutral oil

1 tablespoon minced garlic

4 dried red chiles, torn into bite-sized pieces

Juice of 3 lemons, plus more as needed

1 tablespoon apple cider vinegar

½ teaspoon sugar, plus more as needed

Wash the bitter gourds and cut each in half lengthwise. Use a small metal spoon to remove and discard the seeds, then cut the gourds diagonally into ¼-inch-thick (6 mm) slices.

In a large mixing bowl, combine 2 cups (480 ml) water and the salt. Add the sliced bitter gourd to the water and massage it well, then let it soak for 20 minutes. Drain and rinse the bitter gourd well. Remove excess water using a salad spinner. This removes some of the bitterness.

In a wok over high heat, heat the oil. When the oil is hot, add the garlic and chiles and sauté for about 30 seconds.

Add the bitter gourd and sauté for 2 minutes, then add the lemon juice and vinegar. Stir in the sugar and cook for another 2 to 3 minutes, until the bitter gourd softens and browns.

Taste the gourd. It's meant to be bitter, but if you find the bitterness overpowering, add some more lemon juice or sugar here and continue to fry, then serve.

Chile and Makrut Lime Garlic Bread

MAKES 1 LOAF

Get ready for a garlic bread experience like never before! The combination of makrut lime and chiles adds a refreshing Creole Mauritian kick. This pairs perfectly with my black lentil soup (page 139), balancing the richness of the soup with its zesty and vibrant flavors. But you might end up enjoying the bread all on its own—it's irresistible!

- 1 baguette
- 1 cup (200 g) salted plant-based butter, such as Earth Balance, at room temperature
- 3 large fresh red chiles, finely chopped
- 10 cloves garlic, minced
- ½ cup (20 g) cilantro leaves, roughly chopped
- 6 makrut lime leaves, finely sliced, or the juice from 1 makrut lime or a regular lime
- Salt

Split the baguette in half lengthwise, then slice it into 8 pieces.

In a large skillet over medium heat, melt the butter. Add the chiles, garlic, cilantro, and makrut lime leaves. Sauté until the garlic softens, approximately 1 minute.

Arrange the bread in the skillet cut side down. Give it a gentle press to soak up that flavorful buttery goodness.

Let the bread toast until each slice is gloriously golden brown, about 3 minutes. Flip each slice over to let the other side brown, another 3 minutes, and then serve.

The Creamiest, Cheesiest Vegan Mac 'n' Cheese—Ever!

SERVES 6

Okay, buckle up. I know that every household claims to have the best mac 'n' cheese, but hear me out: this recipe belongs in the mac 'n' cheese hall of fame. Because I'm the mac maestro in my family—the undisputed champion of cheesy goodness.

We've come a long way since the early, underwhelming vegan cheeses. The cheesy vegan flavor I'm about to drop on you with this cashew-based mac will blow your mind; it's downright irresistible.

No need to take my word for it—the queen of hip-hop herself, Remy Ma, couldn't believe this dish was vegan when she tried it on *The Black Vegan Cooking Show*. So get ready for a mac 'n' cheese that might just leave you speechless.

- 1½ cups (180 g) whole raw cashews
- 4 cups (960 ml) hot water
- 12 ounces (340 g) dried macaroni pasta
- 3 cloves garlic
- ¼ cup (35 g) nutritional yeast
- 2½ cups (600 ml) unsweetened plant-based milk
- ½ teaspoon ground turmeric
- ½ teaspoon paprika
- ¼ cup (55 g) salted plant-based butter, such as Earth Balance
- ½ teaspoon onion powder
- 1 teaspoon Dijon mustard
- 1 teaspoon salt, plus more as needed
- ½ teaspoon ground black pepper, plus more as needed
- 4 cups (460 g) shredded vegan cheddar cheese, such as Violife Just Like Colby Jack
- 1 teaspoon salt

In a bowl, soak the cashews in the water for at least 1 hour or up to 3 hours, then drain.

Preheat the oven to 350°F (175°C).

Cook the pasta according to the package directions until al dente or until it retains just a little bite. Drain the pasta in a colander and set aside until ready to use.

Meanwhile, to a high-powered blender, add the soaked cashews, garlic, nutritional yeast, milk, turmeric, paprika, butter, onion powder, mustard, salt, and pepper. Blend until a thick sauce forms. Adjust the consistency with more milk, if desired. Taste and adjust the seasonings.

Pour the creamy cashew sauce into a medium saucepan, add 2 cups (230 g) of the cheese, and warm over low heat, stirring until the cheese is melted.

In a 9 by 13–inch (23 by 33 cm) casserole dish, add the cooked pasta and mix in the cheese sauce. Top with the remaining 2 cups (230 g) cheese.

Cover the dish with aluminum foil. Place the dish on a baking sheet for easy removal and to catch any spills and bake for 30 minutes, then remove the foil and bake for an additional 5 minutes. For extra browning, place the dish under the broiler for 3 to 4 minutes. Watch carefully to avoid burning.

CLOCKWISE FROM TOP LEFT: Chile and Makrut Lime Garlic Bread (page 158), Mango Satini (Mango Chutney; page 224), Spicy Baked Okra Fries (page 155), The Creamiest, Cheesiest Vegan Mac 'n' Cheese—Ever (page 159), Coconut Banana Fritters (page 173), Margose Frire (Stir-Fried Bitter Gourd; page 156)

DESSERTS

I'm not a big baker. When I want to make a dessert, I gravitate toward recipes that are quick and easy. Because when you or your kid feels like something sweet, you want it fast—and it's great to have a few simple, whole ingredients on hand that can satisfy your sweet tooth and keep you from reaching for packaged, unhealthy desserts.

Both Jamaican and Mauritian traditional desserts tend to be simple, built with just a few ingredients. Mauritian desserts often star bananas—cooked in milk, sweetened just right, and flavored with vanilla or cardamom—and mango and tamarind; all ingredients that are readily available on the island, taste great together, and offer a soothing, refreshing finish to a spicy meal. Mauritian desserts also reflect Indian, French, African, and Chinese influences and the island's love for using local ingredients in creative ways. Sweet potatoes are mixed with grated coconut, formed into little cakes, and then fried until golden. The result is a warm, comforting treat that perfectly accompanies a cup of vanilla tea on a lazy afternoon.

In Jamaica, meanwhile, the staple desserts include things like puddings and buns: indulgent treats you make on the weekend and savor over the course of many days. Both cultures' desserts make use of cornmeal, fresh coconut, coconut brown sugar, cinnamon, nutmeg, and vanilla.

Brioche Bread Pudding

SERVES 6

Indulge in the rich heritage of my family's Jamaican bread pudding. Jamaican bread pudding, affectionately called "puddin'" by locals, is much more than just a sweet treat—it's a slice of Jamaican history on a plate. This comforting dessert has its roots in the colonial era but has been lovingly adapted over the years to feature a distinctly Jamaican flair.

Originally, bread pudding came to Jamaica with the British, who brought over their love for this economical dish aimed at using up stale bread. But as with many things in Jamaica, the locals took this simple concept and made it their own, transforming it with the flavors and ingredients available on the island.

Passed down through generations, this classic recipe took a Vegan Soulicious turn under my care. I've veganized it by using plant-based milk, cream, and butter, and we are also using vegan brioche, which takes it to another level. Featured on *Today*, it's a warm hug of tradition with Al Roker's seal of approval.

This Jamaican brioche bread pudding is a delicious twist that keeps all the rich flavors and comforting textures intact while honoring a plant-based lifestyle. Serve this treat with a dollop of coconut whipped cream, caramel sauce, or coconut custard (such as Nature's Charm).

- ½ cup (95 g) coconut brown sugar
- ½ teaspoon ground cinnamon
- ½ teaspoon ground allspice
- ½ teaspoon salt
- 2 tablespoons chia seeds
- 2 cups (480 ml) unsweetened plant-based milk
- 1 cup (240 ml) plant-based cream
- Unsalted plant-based butter, such as Earth Balance, for spreading
- 24 slices vegan brioche or potato bread
- 1 cup (145 g) raisins
- ¼ cup (20 g) shredded coconut (see Note)

In a medium saucepan over medium heat, combine the coconut brown sugar, cinnamon, allspice, salt, chia seeds, milk, and cream. Bring to a simmer and cook until the sugar has dissolved, 4 to 5 minutes. Set aside.

Butter one side of each slice of bread smoothly and cut each slice into 2 triangles.

Generously butter a 1-quart (960 ml) ovenproof baking dish.

Arrange a layer of bread buttered side down in the bottom of the dish. Sprinkle one-quarter of the raisins and one-quarter of the coconut over the bread. Pour one-quarter of the milk mixture over the bread to saturate the bread. Repeat until you have 4 layers. Press down softly, making sure that the bread is absorbing the liquid. Allow the pudding to set for at least 1 hour at room temperature.

Preheat the oven to 375°F (190°C). Bake for 45 minutes, until the pudding is nicely puffed and browned on top. A knife inserted in the center should come out clean. Serve warm, or allow to cool and serve chilled.

You can make this bread pudding ahead of time and keep it covered in the fridge for up to 4 days. It will slice easily while cold; reheat the slices in the microwave or the oven when you're ready to eat.

NOTE

SWAP OPTION: Instead of coconut flakes, try pecans or chocolate chips.

Date Candy Bar

MAKES 10 PIECES

Take your dessert game to a whole new level with these phenomenal candy bars that are so easy to make! In Mauritius, we have an amazing sweet treat called date rolls filled with nuts. Here, I'm putting my own spin on it with a few extra bits and bobs to add some flair. Built on a foundation of tropical Medjool dates and topped with pretzels for extra crunch, these treats are guilt-free and utterly delicious. People always tell me they taste exactly like a Snickers bar, since the texture of a date is shockingly similar to caramel. Even the world-famous rapper Jim Jones couldn't resist these bars when he made a guest appearance on my show, *The Black Vegan Cooking Show*.

10 large Medjool dates, such as Natural Delights

10 small pretzels

1 cup (150 g) salted peanuts or pistachios

¼ cup (60 ml) natural peanut butter (see Notes)

⅓ cup (60 g) vegan chocolate chips, such as Enjoy Life, for melting (see Notes)

1 teaspoon unrefined coconut oil

Salt

Open each date softly with your fingers and remove the pit. Place the dates on a sheet of parchment paper.

Fill each date with a pretzel and fill the holes in the pretzel with nuts. Spread a small spoonful of peanut butter over the top of the pretzel.

To a small bowl, add the chocolate chips and oil. Melt them in the microwave in 30-second intervals, mixing in between each interval (see Notes), until smooth, about 2 minutes total.

Drizzle the stuffed dates with the melted chocolate.

Sprinkle with a generous amount of salt, if you like salty-sweet flavors. And crush some nuts to sprinkle on top as well.

Put the tray of dates in the freezer for 10 to 15 minutes so the chocolate can set. Then store them in the fridge in an airtight container for up to 1 week or the freezer for up to 2 months.

NOTES

PEANUT BUTTER: Opt for drippy natural peanut butter or your favorite nut or seed butter. Whole Foods' 365 brand does the trick. For added texture, use crunchy peanut butter.

MELTING CHOCOLATE: If you don't have a microwave, melt the chocolate on the stove. Place the chocolate in a medium metal bowl, fill a small pot with about 1 inch (2.5 cm) water, and balance the bowl over the pot so that the bottom of the bowl is in the water but does not touch the bottom of the pot. Bring the water to a simmer, then turn off the heat; the residual heat will melt the chocolate.

CHOCOLATE TEXTURE: If your melted chocolate is too thick or not smooth enough, add some more coconut oil.

Mauritian Tropical Fruit Salad

SERVES 4

The *marchand confit*, or "pickled fruit vendors," are a common sight in markets, on streets, and near schools, a testament to the popularity of this snack among Mauritians of all ages. Mauritian fruit confit reflects the island's multicultural heritage, drawing from African, European, Indian, and Chinese cuisines. The vendors sell both pickled fruits and vegetables like jicama, cucumber, green mango, and pineapple in a vinegary brine as well as fruit salads, where the fresh fruit is tossed with chili salt and tamarind sauce, as we are doing here.

In Mauritius, many of us can pick these fruits right from trees in our own backyards. I don't have that luxury in New York, but thankfully we have access to them in our local Caribbean grocery stores and Asian markets, and even through online tropical fruit delivery services that offer nationwide shipping. I have listed some of these services on page 244.

FOR THE FRUIT SALAD:

- 1 pineapple
- 2 semi-ripe mangoes
- ½ small cucumber

FOR THE TAMARIND DRIZZLE:

- 2 tablespoons tamarind paste
- 1 tablespoon coconut brown sugar, plus more as needed
- Pinch of salt, plus more as needed

FOR THE CHILI SALT:

- 1 teaspoon salt
- ½ teaspoon chili powder

TO PREPARE THE FRUIT SALAD:

Peel and chop the pineapple and the mangoes. Use a peeler to slice the cucumber into ribbons.

TO PREPARE THE TAMARIND DRIZZLE:

In a small saucepan over a low/medium heat, combine the tamarind paste, brown sugar, salt, and ⅓ cup (80 ml) water and simmer for 10 to 15 minutes, until the sauce is thick and glossy but pourable. Adjust the sweetness and salt to your liking.

TO PREPARE THE CHILI SALT:

In a small bowl, combine the chili powder and salt.

TO SERVE:

On a plate, arrange the fruit and cucumber ribbons. Sprinkle with the chili salt and drizzle with the tamarind sauce.

For the freshest and most vibrant taste, enjoy immediately. If you have leftovers, store them covered in an airtight container in the refrigerator for up to 3 days, but keep in mind that the taste and texture may change slightly.

Coconut Banana Fritters

SERVES 4

These crunchy fried bananas coated in coconut batter are seriously addictive! From the moment you hear them sizzling in the frying pan and smell their irresistible aroma, you'll be hooked. And just wait until you taste them! The delightful crunch of the batter and the burst of sweetness from ripe bananas are just too good to resist—I can't help but keep going back for more. It's as if these golden-brown fritters offer a little piece of tropical heaven in every bite.

1⅓ cups (165 g) all-purpose flour

⅔ cup (80 g) coconut flour (see Note)

2 tablespoons sugar

½ teaspoon salt

½ teaspoon ground nutmeg

½ teaspoon ground cinnamon

1½ teaspoons baking powder

Neutral oil, for frying

6 bananas (on the riper side)

Vegan vanilla ice cream, such as Oatly, for serving (optional)

1 tablespoon unsweetened coconut flakes, for garnish

Agave or honey, for drizzling

Chocolate sauce, for drizzling (optional)

In a mixing bowl, whisk ⅔ cup (80 g) of the all-purpose flour with the coconut flour, sugar, salt, nutmeg, cinnamon, and baking powder. Slowly whisk in 2 cups (480 ml) water until smooth. The mixture should look like a thick pancake batter. Let it rest at least 20 minutes.

Meanwhile, pour oil into a large pot until it's 3 inches (7.5 cm) deep and heat the oil to 375°F (190°C) when measured with a deep-fry thermometer. Set a cooling rack on a baking sheet.

Slice the bananas in half crosswise.

Put the remaining ⅔ cup (80 g) of the all-purpose flour in a bowl and dredge the sliced bananas in the flour.

Drop a few of the floured banana pieces in the batter and turn to coat. Carefully lower them into the oil. Fry the bananas until they are a deep golden brown, 7 to 10 minutes, then use a slotted spoon to lift them to the cooling rack. Scoop out and discard any bits of fried batter remaining in the oil before adding the next batch Repeat until all the pieces have been fried.

Divide the banana fritters among 4 bowls and serve with a scoop of ice cream, if using, a sprinkle of coconut flakes, and drizzles of agave or honey and chocolate sauce, if desired.

NOTE

BRING THE CRUNCH: If you're looking for an extra-crunchy crust, use coconut flour as called for in the recipe above. However, if you prefer a softer bite, substitute rice flour. Experiment with both options (one or the other—don't use a mix of the two) to find the perfect crust for your culinary creations!

La Daube Banane (Spiced Sweet and Sticky Plantains)

SERVES 6

Mauritius and the Seychelles are neighboring islands. The closeness between the islands is also reflected in their food, which shares many similarities and flavors. I spent some time in the Seychelles as my stepfather, France, is from there. His aunt Claire, whom I came to consider my aunt as well, used to treat us to something truly special—la daube banane, or "banana stew," made with ripe plantains, vanilla, cinnamon, and coconut straight from the backyard. This family favorite traditionally makes use of abundant local produce, but you'll love it even if you don't have your own coconut tree.

Though the Mauritian name for this stew includes the word "banana," in this recipe I use plantains. Plantains and bananas may look similar, but they have very noticeable differences in texture and size. Plantains tend to be larger, starchier, and firmer in texture than bananas.

- 3 large, ripe plantains
- 3 cinnamon sticks
- 3 tablespoons coconut brown sugar
- 1 teaspoon salt
- 1 teaspoon ground nutmeg
- 1 vanilla bean pod, split (see Notes)
- 1 (13½-ounce/400 ml) can unsweetened coconut milk

Peel the plantains. Cut each one into 4 pieces by cutting in half first crosswise, then lengthwise.

To a large pot, add the cinnamon sticks. Layer the cut plantains on top of the cinnamon sticks, ensuring that the cut side is facing up. Sprinkle the cut plantains with the brown sugar, salt, and nutmeg. Add the split vanilla pod, then pour in the coconut milk.

Place the pot over high heat, bring to a boil, and cook uncovered for 10 minutes. Reduce the heat to low and simmer for 35 minutes, covered, allowing the flavors to meld and the plantains to absorb the infused coconut milk.

Once cooked, turn off the heat and let it sit for a few minutes. Check if the plantains are ready by inserting a fork into the middle of one; it should be tender. Remove the vanilla bean pod and serve hot. This dessert can be stored in the fridge in an airtight container for up to 2 days.

NOTES

VANILLA SUBSTITUTION: No vanilla beans on hand? Not to worry! Substitute 1 teaspoon of vanilla extract for a convenient and equally flavorful alternative.

VANILLA BEAN PREP: When working with vanilla beans, enhance your dish by splitting the pod in two and scraping the seeds, then add both the seeds and pod to the dish.

1 (11-ounce/325 g) can sweetened condensed coconut milk, such as Nature's Charm

3 cardamom pods

3 cups (255 g) shredded coconut

1 teaspoon vanilla extract, almond extract, or rose water

1 or 2 drops natural food coloring in red, green, or yellow

In a saucepan over medium heat, combine the condensed milk and cardamom pods. Heat for about 5 minutes, to infuse the cardamom into the milk. Remove the cardamom pods from the milk and discard.

Stir the shredded coconut into the condensed milk and cook until it thickens, about 5 minutes. When your spoon leaves a clean path along the bottom of the pan, remove the pan from the heat.

Add the extract or rose water and a few drops of your preferred food coloring. Mix well, ensuring the color is evenly distributed.

It's time to shape the gâteaux koko. Use an ice-cream scoop to form balls about 1½ inches (4 cm) in diameter (see Note). Drop the balls onto a tray lined with parchment paper, spaced about 2 inches (5 cm) apart.

Place the tray in the freezer for about 15 minutes for the gâteaux koko to set, then serve. Store any leftovers in an airtight container for up to 2 days.

NOTE

NO ICE-CREAM SCOOP? NO PROBLEM! For an effortless "drop" of gâteaux koko, grab two tablespoons. Use one tablespoon to scoop up the mixture and then gently push it onto the tray with the back of the other tablespoon. This easy work-around ensures uniform portions without the need for a specialized scoop.

My Famous Three-Ingredient Mango Ice Cream

SERVES 8

Get ready to savor the dessert that took the internet by storm—my very own mango ice cream sensation with more than four million views on Instagram! Your love and excitement made this dish a sweet triumph, but I owe this one to my mum, who used to make mango ice cream for me all the time.

Ripe, juicy mangoes meet coconut cream in a dessert that has captured the hearts of millions. Each scoop is a vibrant tropical treat—and the best part is that you can whip up the magic with just a few simple ingredients. No ice cream machine needed!

4 to 6 fresh mangoes, or 2¼ cups (530 ml) fresh mango pulp or puree (see Notes)

2¼ cups (530 ml) canned coconut or oat whipping cream, chilled (see Notes)

1½ cups (360 ml) sweetened condensed coconut milk, such as Nature's Charm

Peel and deseed the mangoes. In a blender, puree them until smooth; you should have about 2¼ cups (530 ml) mango puree. Set aside.

In a stand mixer with the whisk attachment, whip the coconut cream until soft peaks form. Add the condensed coconut milk and whisk for another minute until well combined.

Gradually add the mango puree to the whipped cream in ½-cup (120 ml) increments, whisking after each addition for a smooth blend. Mix just until the mango is incorporated, being careful not to overmix.

Pour the mixture into a parchment-lined, freezer-friendly container.

Cover the container and freeze for at least 5 hours, until the ice cream is set (see Notes).

Before serving, remove the ice cream from the freezer 15 minutes in advance to allow it to thaw slightly. For ease of serving, use a hot ice-cream scoop (see Notes).

NOTES

CHOOSING MANGOES: For the ultimate flavor experience, opt for fresh Alphonso mangoes if available. If not, use Alphonso mango pulp. The sweet, aromatic characteristics of Alphonso mangoes truly enhance the taste of this ice cream.

CHILLING COCONUT: Refrigerate the cans of coconut whipping cream overnight to ensure the ice cream has a velvety, creamy consistency. Consider keeping a few cans in the fridge regularly for convenient and quick ice-cream making!

MANGO RIBBONS: For extra mango flavor, swirl additional mango pulp through the ice cream after placing the ice cream into your freezer-friendly container.

SIMPLE SCOOPING: Using a warmed ice-cream scoop will make scooping easier and elevate your presentation. Submerge your ice-cream scoop in a pot of boiled water for a few minutes before using.

Poudine Maïs (Polenta Pudding)

SERVES 8

This classic Mauritian dessert is effortlessly simple to make, perfect for enjoying alongside a warm cup of tea. Known as "poudine maïs" in French, it became popular in Mauritius in the 1960s and was frequently sold by street vendors. Today, it's still a beloved dessert that is enjoyed all year round, but especially during the holidays. As a child, I always looked forward to getting a slice at Easter.

Unlike similar Caribbean dishes such as "cornmeal pone," which are typically baked, this Mauritian pudding is gently cooked on the stovetop over low heat, allowing the flavors to meld and develop to perfection. The result is a creamy, dense dessert that's best enjoyed cold. While the classic recipe calls for whole milk, my vegan twist uses oat milk for a creamy and guilt-free indulgence.

Experience the ease and yumminess of this cherished Mauritian dessert, celebrating simplicity, tradition, and the joy of good food.

- 1 cup (500 ml) oat milk
- 1⅔ cups (300 g) polenta (cornmeal)
- 1 teaspoon vanilla extract
- ½ cup (125 g) coconut brown sugar
- ¼ cup (20 g) grated coconut, plus more for sprinkling
- ¼ cup (35 g) raisins (optional)
- 1 tablespoon unsalted plant-based butter, such as Earth Balance
- Crushed pistachios, for garnish
- Crushed edible dried rose petals, for garnish

In a saucepan over medium heat, heat the milk and polenta, stirring continuously to prevent burning or sticking to the pan, for about 15 minutes, until thickened.

Add the vanilla extract and continue cooking until all the liquid has evaporated and the polenta has softened, about 15 minutes more.

Add the sugar, grated coconut, and raisins, if using, and mix well.

Grease a round glass dish 10 inches (26 cm) in diameter with the butter. Pour the mixture into the dish and allow it to set in the fridge for a minimum of 2 hours, or until firm. Traditionally, this pudding is set in a square dish, but I use a round glass bowl, as I like to turn the pudding upside down once it's set and sprinkle a little extra coconut, crushed pistachios, and crushed dried rose petals over the top.

Once the pudding has set, cut it into slices and serve. Leftovers can be kept in an airtight container in the fridge for about a week.

Sticky Toffee Pudding

SERVES 8

One of my favorite desserts from my time in London was sticky toffee pudding, a delicacy that involved a warm, moist sponge cake made with finely chopped dates, covered in toffee sauce and served with cream.

What made sticky toffee pudding extra special for me was its resemblance to the puddings my grandma Bernice used to whip up back in Jamaica. Inspired by her culinary legacy of indulgent yet wholesome desserts, I've veganized the elusive sticky toffee pudding of my London days! The rich, gooey goodness, the sweet nostalgia, all without a hint of animal products.

FOR THE PUDDING:

- 1 (8-ounce/250 g) box Medjool dates (12 to 15 dates), such as Natural Delights, pitted
- ½ cup (120 ml) unsweetened plant-based milk
- 2 teaspoons baking powder
- 1 teaspoon vanilla extract
- ¼ teaspoon salt
- ¾ cup (145 g) coconut brown sugar
- 2 tablespoons golden syrup, such as Lyle's
- ½ cup (115 g) unsalted plant-based butter, such as Earth Balance, softened
- 1¼ cup (155 g) self-rising flour

FOR THE TOFFEE SAUCE:

- ¼ cup (55 g) unsalted plant-based butter, such as Earth Balance
- ¾ cup (145 g) coconut brown sugar
- 1 tablespoon cornstarch
- 1 tablespoon golden syrup
- 1 teaspoon vanilla extract
- 1 cup (240 ml) plant-based cream

FOR SERVING:

- Oat or soy heavy cream

TO PREPARE THE PUDDING:

Preheat the oven to 350°F (175°C).

To a small saucepan over low heat, add the dates and enough water to cover. Bring to a gentle simmer and cook until the dates soften and absorb some water, about 20 minutes. Drain the dates and place them in a blender or food processor with the milk. Puree until you achieve a smooth consistency.

In a mixing bowl, combine the date mixture with the baking powder, vanilla extract, salt, brown sugar, golden syrup, and butter. Mix well. Gradually fold in the self-rising flour until you have a smooth batter.

Grease and flour a medium baking tin, preferably 10 by 7 inches (25 by 18 cm). Pour the pudding batter into the tin and bake for 30 to 35 minutes, until the pudding is golden brown and firm. A knife inserted into the center should come out clean.

Remove the pudding from the oven and allow it to cool slightly while you prepare the toffee sauce.

TO PREPARE THE TOFFEE SAUCE:

In a saucepan over medium heat, melt the butter. Stir in the brown sugar, cornstarch, golden syrup, vanilla extract, and cream. Bring the mixture to a gentle boil, stirring continuously, and let it simmer for 2 to 3 minutes, until the sauce thickens. Remove from the heat.

TO ASSEMBLE AND SERVE:

Poke holes in the warm pudding using a fork or skewer. Pour a generous amount of the warm toffee sauce over the pudding, allowing it to seep into the holes. Reserve some toffee sauce for serving.

Serve generous slices of the pudding drizzled with extra toffee sauce and some cream.

Mauritian Aloudas (Rose and Mint Ice Cream Floats)

SERVES 2

Dive into the creamy, dreamy, and downright delightful world of alouda—a dessert superstar straight from the heart of Mauritius. One of the most popular drinks in Mauritius, alouda is often sold at markets and street food stalls. This refreshing childhood favorite combines the playful chewiness of noodles and basil seeds with ice cream to create the perfect treat for the sizzling Mauritian heat. You can incorporate any of your favorite flavors and toppings, as I have done here: One uses mint syrup and rose petals, the other has rose syrup and pistachios.

- 2 tablespoons sweet basil seeds or chia seeds
- ½ (16-ounce/500 g) pack falooda sev (thin vermicelli noodles – available in Indian grocery stores)
- 2 scoops vegan vanilla ice cream
- 2 tablespoons (60 ml) rose syrup
- 2 tablespoons (60 ml) mint syrup
- 1 cup (240 ml) unsweetened plant-based milk
- 1 tablespoon pistachios, crushed, for garnish
- 1 tablespoon edible dried rose petals, for garnish

In a small bowl, soak the sweet basil seeds in ½ cup (120 ml) water for about 15 minutes, or until they double in size.

In a pot, boil 3 cups (720 ml) water. Cut the vermicelli noodles into 2-inch (5 cm) pieces and cook them according to package instructions. Drain the cooked noodles in a colander, rinse them under cold water, and set aside.

Assemble the drinks in 2 tall glasses: In the first glass, layer a scoop of ice cream, 1 tablespoon soaked sweet basil seeds, 1 tablespoon cooked noodles, and 1 tablespoon rose syrup.

In the second glass, layer 1 tablespoon soaked sweet basil seeds, a scoop of ice cream, 1 tablespoon cooked noodles, and 1 tablespoon mint syrup.

Pour ½ cup (120 ml) milk into each glass. Stir gently to combine the noodles, syrup, and milk. Garnish the glass with the rose syrup with pistachios and the glass with the mint syrup with rose petals. Serve immediately.

GIFT SHOP
GIFT SHOP
Dole
PREMIUM BANANAS
PLANTAIN
Patrona
The one and only
CHULA
PLANTAINS
Sweet cooked or ripe!
PRODUCT OF GUATEMALA
HANDLE WITH CARE
NET WEIGHT 50 LB (22.68 KG)
PRODUCT OF GUATEMALA
CHULA
PLANTAINS
Dole
PREMIUM BANANAS
Dole
Kapi

ISLAND DRINKS

In Jamaican and Mauritian culture, we have a drink for every purpose. Whether you're looking for a sweet treat or a boozy cocktail to enjoy on the weekends; a calming herbal tea to help you kick that pesky cold; or a pick-me-up shot to get your day going, this section has the beverage for you.

In a Jamaican-Mauritian household, pills aren't the first solution when someone feels under the weather. As islanders, my parents swore by the holistic approach, finding remedies from nature.

Tea is a big part of Jamaican culture, in particular. From comforting mugs of chocolate tea to spicy cups of ginger tea, we all grew up believing that teas were like magic elixirs for any kind of sickness. Honestly, there's a lot of truth to that. The teas in this section are tasty and feel like a hug in a cup!

You'll also find recipes for some of my favorite juices. Call me the Juicing Queen, because I'm all about squeezing the good stuff out of every fruit and veggie—and tossing in some wild cards for kicks. Daily juicing is my thing! And it's not just carrots and apples in my kingdom. I'll throw in everything but the kitchen sink to make taste bud–rocking juices and shots. These daily shots are natural boosters for health and immunity, made with a sprinkle of love. I whip up batches and stash them in the fridge—a little island healing, ready to go!

FROM LEFT TO RIGHT: Creole Rum Passion Cocktail (page 191), Jamaican Guinness Punch (page 190), Jamaican Sorrel (Hibiscus Drink; page 193) Tropical Sea Moss Slammer (page 191)

Jamaican Guinness Punch

SERVES 4 TO 6

Jamaicans love Guinness punch. This rich, malty-sweet alcoholic beverage has notes of coffee and chocolate and traditionally stars condensed cow's milk. I can already hear all my fellow islanders protesting: "Dairy-free Guinness punch, you say?"

Yes! I'll admit that veganizing Guinness punch was quite the challenge, which was solved only after I started making my own condensed milk (page 228). But then Nature's Charm blessed us with condensed oat milk—a true game-changer, making it easier than ever to whip up a batch of vegan Guinness punch! Oh, how I missed this punch!

- 1½ cups (360 ml) Guinness beer (see Notes)
- 1 cup (240 ml) oat or almond milk
- 1 teaspoon vanilla extract
- ¼ teaspoon freshly grated nutmeg, plus more for serving
- ⅛ teaspoon ground cinnamon
- ½ cup (120 ml) condensed oat milk, homemade (see page 228) or Nature's Charm
- 3 drops angostura bitters (optional, see Notes)
- Ice cubes

In a bowl, whisk together the beer, milk, vanilla extract, nutmeg, cinnamon, condensed milk, and angostura bitters, if using. You can also use a blender to mix them for a foamier texture.

Serve over ice with a sprinkle of nutmeg (see Notes). Store leftovers in an airtight container in the fridge for up to 2 days.

NOTES

MAKE IT A MOCKTAIL: If you want to make it nonalcoholic, use malta (a lightly carbonated drink brewed from barley, hops, and water) instead of Guinness.

CUSTOMIZE YOUR PUNCH: For a more bitter punch, add an extra ½ cup (120 ml) Guinness. For an extra kick, add a splash of rum. For an extra layer of flavor, add a dash of angostura bitters. It's optional but worth trying!

Creole Rum Passion Cocktail

MAKES 1 COCKTAIL

Rum is the prized drink of Mauritius. There are numerous distilleries on the island thanks to the abundant sugarcane fields, and vanilla rum is an especially big deal. My Mauritian rum cocktail is a fusion of rich island flavors, evoking the sweetness of passion fruit and a whiff of vanilla bean with each sip. Cheers to a tropical escape!

- 1 lime, halved
- 9 fresh basil leaves, 6 leaves finely chopped
- 4 tablespoons (55 g) brown sugar
- 1 teaspoon raw sugar
- 1 whole fresh passion fruit, halved, pulp and seeds scooped out
- 1 ounce (45 ml) Chamarel white rum or other vanilla-based white rum
- Ice cubes

Squeeze the juice of one-half lime onto a small plate.

In another shallow dish, mix together the chopped basil and brown sugar until evenly combined.

Take a cocktail glass and dip the rim into the lime juice, making sure the entire rim is evenly moistened. Immediately dip the moistened rim into the brown sugar and basil mixture. Rotate the glass to ensure the rim is evenly coated. Gently shake off any excess mixture. Let the rim set for a few minutes before pouring your drink into the glass.

In a mixing glass, add the juice of the remaining one-half lime, the whole basil leaves, raw sugar, and passion fruit. Muddle these together until well mixed and the sugar dissolves. Pour in the rum, add some ice, and give it a good stir. Pour the drink into the prepared cocktail glass.

Tropical Sea Moss Slammer

MAKES 1 SMOOTHIE

Ready to whip up something super refreshing, healthy, and totally tropical? This smoothie is a real game-changer, blending up sea moss gel with fruity favorites to kick-start your day or give you that perfect afternoon boost. Sea moss is packed with minerals and good stuff to keep your digestion and skin feeling awesome.

- ¾ cup (180 ml) flavorless, organic sea moss gel, such as Keymoss Sea Moss
- 2 cups (330 g) frozen mango cubes
- 1 cup (165 g) frozen pineapple cubes
- 1 cup (240 ml) canned unsweetened coconut milk
- Toasted coconut, for garnish (optional)

To a blender, add the sea moss gel, mango, pineapple, and coconut milk and blend until smooth.

Serve in a glass and garnish with toasted coconut, if desired.

Jamaican Sorrel (Hibiscus Drink)

SERVES 10

Sorrel is a drink made from a type of hibiscus flower known as sorrel or roselle. This drink has its roots in West Africa; it made its way abroad during the transatlantic slave trade and is now the traditional Christmas beverage in Jamaica. It also happens to be a naturally healthy wonder: Full of antioxidants and vitamins, it fights inflammation, keeps the heart happy, and helps with digestion.

3 cups (150 g) dried or fresh sorrel (hibiscus), rinsed with cold water

1¾ cups (335 g) washed, unpeeled, grated fresh ginger

10 whole cloves

10 allspice berries, roughly crushed, or 1 teaspoon ground allspice

2 cups (380 g) coconut brown sugar

Ice cubes

In a 5-quart (4.7 L) pot, bring 3 quarts (2.8 L) water to a boil. Add the sorrel, ginger, cloves, and allspice and boil until the sorrel begins to plump and swell, about 8 minutes.

Remove from heat, add the brown sugar, and let stand until cooled, then continue to steep in an airtight vessel in the fridge for at least 8 hours or up to 3 days.

Strain the liquid through a fine-mesh strainer into a large pitcher. The drink should be completely clear of any bits and pieces; if needed, strain again.

Chill until ready to drink. Serve over ice.

Tamarind Lemonade

SERVES 2

I've taken a killer tamarind lemonade recipe from Mauritius and tweaked it to make it super easy and quick—perfect for those blazing-hot days when you need something truly refreshing. Since I'm all about that heat, I throw in a bit of cayenne to spice things up. But hey, if spicy isn't your jam, feel free to skip it. No hard feelings!

7 lemons

3 tablespoons tamarind paste, plus more as needed

3 teaspoons agave, plus more as needed

1 teaspoon ground ginger (or 1 tablespoon freshly grated ginger for more zing)

½ teaspoon ground cardamom

1 teaspoon cayenne pepper (optional)

4 to 6 cups (946 ml to 1.4 L) chilled water

Ice cubes

Fresh mint sprigs

Squeeze the juice from 6 lemons. To maximize juice yield, roll the lemons on your countertop with your palm before cutting and squeezing them.

Thinly slice the remaining lemon for garnish. Set aside.

In a large jar or pitcher, combine the lemon juice and 3 tablespoons of the tamarind paste. Add the agave and whisk thoroughly, until the agave is completely dissolved.

Add the ginger, cardamom, and cayenne, if using.

Pour the chilled water into the mixture. Add more or less, depending on how concentrated you prefer your lemonade. Give it a taste; add more tamarind or agave until it's how you like it. (I use up to ½ cup/120 ml tamarind, but how much depends on the puree's concentration and your taste preference.)

Add the reserved lemon slices and serve over ice cubes, garnished with fresh mint.

TEA SOOTHES THE SOUL

CLOCKWISE FROM TOP LEFT: Galangal Blood Orange Tea (page 198), Ginger Turmeric Tea (page 200), Jamaican Chocolate Tea (page 201), Grandma Bernice's Jamaican Pineapple-Skin Tea (page 202)

Galangal Blood Orange Tea

MAKES 6 CUPS (1.4 L)

My family in Jamaica used to make this tea with fresh blood oranges from a tree in the backyard. They used ginger in this recipe, but I've swapped it out for galangal, which looks very similar but has a spicier, more intense kick. You can find it in most Asian grocery stores.

Fun fact: galangal might not just spice up your recipes; it can also boost male fertility! Let's add a pinch of fun and flavor to the kitchen—you might just be cooking up more than a delicious cup of tea!

- 3½ ounces (100 g) unpeeled, chopped fresh galangal
- 1 teaspoon ground black pepper
- 1 teaspoon ground turmeric
- 2 cinnamon sticks
- 2 blood oranges, sliced
- Sweetener such as agave or coconut brown sugar

In a large pot, combine the galangal, black pepper, turmeric, cinnamon sticks, and blood oranges. Add water to fill the pot, about 8 cups (2 L). Place the pot on the stove over medium-high heat and bring to a boil.

Reduce the heat to low and simmer for 1 hour.

Strain using a fine-mesh sieve or cheesecloth.

Serve hot or cold, with as much sweetener as your heart desires.

NOTES

WHY YOU SHOULD USE TURMERIC AND BLACK PEPPER TOGETHER

Turmeric and black pepper make a dynamic duo. When you add black pepper to turmeric, a compound called piperine boosts the bioavailability and effectiveness of turmeric's active compound, curcumin, by up to 2,000 percent. Together, these spices maximize each other's health benefits.

ANTI-INFLAMMATORY BUDDIES: These spices make a potent anti-inflammatory combo, beneficial for conditions like arthritis.

ANTIOXIDANT SUPPORT: The combo is packed with antioxidants, combating oxidative stress in your body.

DIGESTIVE HEALTH: Turmeric aids digestion, while black pepper stimulates stomach acid production.

POTENTIAL CANCER PREVENTION: Studies suggest that the curcumin-piperine combo may have anti-cancer properties.

BLOOD SUGAR BALANCE: Turmeric and black pepper may help regulate blood sugar levels.

HEART HEALTH: Both contribute to cardiovascular health, with curcumin showing potential in lowering cholesterol.

Ginger Turmeric Tea

MAKES 6 CUPS (1.6 L)

This ginger tea is a lovely blend of warmth, spice, and a hint of citrus—perfect for chilly days or whenever you need a soothing, flavorful cup! When I was growing up, my father would brew a fresh pot of ginger tea each morning. He followed this wonderful ritual religiously, and now I've embraced the tradition. It's a comforting routine that connects me to my roots and brings a sense of warmth to each day. Plus, this tea has many healing properties: ginger can help fight nausea, regulate digestion, and soothe inflammation.

- 1 (3.5-ounce/100 g) piece peeled fresh ginger, cut into smaller chunks (see Note)
- 1 teaspoon ground black pepper
- ½ teaspoon ground turmeric
- 2 star anise
- 2 lemons, sliced, plus additional slices for garnish
- 4 cinnamon sticks
- Sweetener, such as agave or coconut brown sugar (optional)

In a medium pot, combine the ginger, pepper, turmeric, star anise, lemon slices (with skin on), and cinnamon sticks. Add water to fill the pot, about 8 cups (2 L). Place the pot on the stove over medium-high heat and bring to a boil.

Reduce the heat to low and let the mixture simmer for about 30 minutes. The longer it simmers, the spicier your tea will be. Adjust the cooking time to suit your taste. As the tea simmers, taste it and add more water if needed.

Turn off the heat and strain the tea using a fine-mesh sieve or cheesecloth. Get rid of all those chunky bits; we want a smooth cup of goodness.

If you have a sweet tooth, stir in your favorite sweetener. Make it just right for you!

Serve steaming hot with lemon slices.

NOTE

AMP IT UP: For a stronger tea, grate the ginger instead of cutting it into chunks. This is actually how I prepare my tea, as I like it really spicy and fiery. Don't be shy with your ginger; the more the merrier!

Jamaican Chocolate Tea

MAKES 2 CUPS (480 ML)

Cacao tea is an ancient elixir that was revered by the Mayan and Aztec civilizations for its mood-boosting properties. This Jamaican version—which my grandmother used to make for me—offers a departure from the usual packaged hot cocoa. It's usually prepared by grating cacao balls made from a mixture of cacao powder and cacao butter, giving the tea a rich flavor, but in a pinch you can use cocoa powder. Either way, the warming spices will bring your hot chocolate experience to the next level.

Crafted with care and authenticity, my recipe stands out with its simplicity and lack of additives, preservatives, or unnatural ingredients. This comforting cup of tea, with its notes of cinnamon, nutmeg, and bay leaf, tastes better than store-bought cocoa and will connect you to a time-honored legacy. And, because cacao is packed with antioxidants, this chocolatey treat is also great for your heart, mood, and brain.

Enhance your experience by listening to Bob Marley while you prepare this tea.

1 (1-ounce/28 g) cacao ball, or 6 to 8 tablespoons (48 to 64 g) raw organic cocoa powder

1 teaspoon ground cinnamon

1 teaspoon freshly grated nutmeg, plus more for garnish

1 bay leaf

1 (13½-ounce/400 ml) can unsweetened coconut milk

2 or 3 tablespoons agave for sweetness (optional)

In a small pot over high heat, bring 2 cups (240 ml) water to a boil. Grate the cacao ball into the pot or add the cocoa powder.

Add the cinnamon, nutmeg, and bay leaf. Cover and simmer over low heat for 10 minutes.

Stir in the coconut milk.

Adjust the sweetness by adding agave to taste, if desired. Mix well and let the tea simmer for an additional 2 to 3 minutes.

Remove the bay leaf before serving in a big mug; finish with a little freshly grated nutmeg on top.

Grandma Bernice's Jamaican Pineapple-Skin Tea

SERVES 6

Did you know that you can turn pineapple skin into a wellness elixir? You see, pineapple skin packs a punch, with high levels of bromelain, a superstar enzyme. This compound combats inflammation and works wonders on your menstrual cycle. From easing discomfort to promoting smooth blood circulation, consider this tea your secret ally during your period. But this delicious herbal tea's benefits don't stop at period pain—its many healing properties make it a drink the whole family can enjoy.

The potential benefits are just about endless: Bromelain may also speed up healing and break food down in your digestive tract, ensuring that everything in your gut is operating smoothly. The minerals in pineapple skin act as a natural diuretic, helping your body kick out toxins and leaving your kidneys feeling refreshed. Full of antioxidants, flavonoids, and phenolic acids, pineapple peel also helps your body defend against infections.

Peel, crown, and scraps of 1 pineapple (everything but the flesh – see Notes)

2 cinnamon sticks

1 lemon, sliced, skin on

1 tablespoon peeled, grated fresh turmeric, or 1 teaspoon ground turmeric (see Notes)

¼ cup (50 g) grated fresh ginger (see Notes)

½ teaspoon cayenne pepper

2 sprigs rosemary, thyme, or basil

2 oranges, sliced, skin on

Sweetener such as agave or coconut brown sugar (optional)

In a large pot, combine the pineapple, cinnamon sticks, lemon, turmeric, ginger, cayenne, rosemary, and oranges. Add water to fill the pot, about 8 cups (2 L). Place the pot on the stove over medium heat and bring to a boil.

Reduce the heat to low and simmer for at least 2 hours – the longer it simmers, the more flavorful it will become.

Pour the contents of the pot through a sieve to collect the liquid. Press down on the pineapple skins with the back of a spoon or a ladle to squeeze out all the juice. This ensures that you get every bit of flavor and nutrients from the skins.

If you prefer a sweeter tea, stir in some agave or coconut brown sugar while the tea is still warm.

Serve the tea hot, or let it cool and serve it chilled as a refreshing drink.

NOTES

SCRUB AWAY: It's essential to clean the pineapple skin thoroughly. Do this by scrubbing the pineapple with a vegetable brush.

ROOT PREP: Prepare the ginger and turmeric roots by washing and peeling them, then grate them with a garlic grating dish or a fine grater. Wear gloves for this step, as the turmeric WILL stain your skin.

Storage: Store the leftover pineapple-skin tea in a glass container in the refrigerator for up to 3 days.

FRESH JUICE

FROM LEFT TO RIGHT:
Sweet Potato Juice (page 206), Sea Moss Watermelon Juice (page 207), Ugo Verde (Green Juice; page 210), Carrot Juice (page 211)

Sweet Potato Juice

SERVES 1

Sweet potato, my friend! I know, it's not the usual juicing suspect, but team it up with pear, apple, and a sprinkle of cinnamon, and it'll blow your mind.

Despite its sweet name, sweet potato juice is low in sugar (but high in goodness)! It is a vitamin A powerhouse, defending your heart, keeping cancer at bay, and giving your brain a longevity boost. The potassium and magnesium in sweet potato juice can help ease your stress, plus potassium is great for cramp relief. It's also rich in fiber, cleaning your digestive tract and keeping heartburn at bay. For moms-to-be, it's packed with folate for healthy cell and tissue growth.

- 2 medium unpeeled, organic sweet potatoes
- 1 unpeeled pear
- 1 unpeeled red apple
- ¼ teaspoon ground cinnamon

EQUIPMENT:

Juicer (see page 29)

Juice the sweet potatoes, pear, and apple according to your juicer's guidelines. You can freeze the pulp to use in baking muffins, or simply put in the compost. Whisk in the cinnamon for that perfect kick.

Drink this juice right off the bat, or store it in the fridge for up to a day. Waiting too long is like letting its precious nutrients sneak out the back door!

Sea Moss Watermelon Juice

SERVES 4

My dad was obsessed with watermelon, and this was his recipe! It comes together quickly with fresh limes and sea moss gel over ice—a classic move.

Sea moss and watermelon are the ultimate healthy power duo; sea moss brings a ton of minerals, and watermelon offers a hydration kick. Together, they're your go-to for glowing skin, healthy joints, and an energy boost. Hydrate and feel great!

This juice also makes a perfect gym companion. Loaded with water, antioxidants, and amino acids, it's practically a workout BFF. It's also full of potassium, the cramp-fighting superhero we all need after the gym.

- 1 small seedless watermelon
- 1 lime
- 2 teaspoons flavorless, organic sea moss gel, such as Keymoss Sea Moss
- Fresh mint, for garnish (optional)

EQUIPMENT:

Juicer (see page 29)

Remove the rinds from the watermelon and lime and juice the fruit flesh with a juicer.

Stir the sea moss gel into your juice and garnish with fresh mint, if desired.

Dispose of the pulp in your compost bin. You can store any leftover juice in a glass airtight container in the refrigerator for up to 3 days.

Ugo Verde (Green Juice)

SERVES 1

I stumbled upon this gem in Mexico, and it's been a staple in my kitchen ever since. The secret? Cactus!

Cactus has a grassy taste like wheatgrass. You can find whole cactus pads at most Latin American grocery stores. Their juice can help manage blood sugar levels, reduce inflammation, and boost the immune system.

1 cactus pad (about 2 ounces/55 g), needles removed, washed, and chopped

1 (½-inch/12 mm) piece unpeeled fresh ginger

2 cups (330 g) chunked unpeeled pineapple

1 whole unpeeled green apple

1 unpeeled lime

¼ cup (9 g) chopped parsley

EQUIPMENT:

Juicer (see page 29)

Toss the cactus pad, ginger, pineapple, apple, lime, and parsley in a juicer, juice away, and let the fiesta begin!

Dispose of the pulp in your compost bin. You can store any leftover juice in a glass airtight container in the refrigerator for up to 3 days.

Carrot Juice

SERVES 4 TO 6

Carrot juice is a classic Jamaican beverage. And no, it's not just simply carrots put through a juicer. It's thick and rich, almost like a dessert, and it features aromatic spices, condensed milk, and sometimes even Guinness. People get really competitive about their recipes for it—if you have guests over, they'll definitely want to try *your* carrot juice to see if it matches up to their family's recipe. You wouldn't believe the showdown the men in my family had over making carrot juice on Sundays—it was truly an epic battle! But let me tell you, my dad's twist on carrot juice emerged as the undeniable champion. There's just something about my family's recipes, and this one is a real gem.

Below I'll spill the beans (or, as you might rightly point out, the carrots) on how to make my dad's victorious carrot juice! Of course, I've added my own twist by veganizing it, thanks to Nature's Charm's vegan condensed milk, and I think my dad would be very proud of this recipe.

2 pounds (910 g) carrots (see Notes)

½ teaspoon grated fresh ginger (or more according to preference)

2 cups (480 ml) unsweetened plant-based milk

1 cup (240 ml) vegan condensed milk, homemade (see page 228) or Nature's Charm

1 (12.2-ounce/360 ml) can coconut evaporated milk, such as Nature's Charm

½ teaspoon ground nutmeg

½ teaspoon ground cinnamon

1 teaspoon vanilla extract

1 (12-ounce/350 ml) bottle malta (see Notes)

EQUIPMENT:

Juicer (see page 29)

Wash and peel the carrots. Cut them into smaller pieces for easier juicing.

Using a juicer, juice the carrots and ginger. Pour the juice into a tall glass bottle. Reserve the pulp for another use. Alternatively, if you do not have a juicer, blend the carrots and ginger in a blender and strain the pulp from the mixture with a fine-mesh strainer or cheesecloth.

Add the milk, condensed milk, evaporated milk, nutmeg, cinnamon, vanilla extract, and malta to the carrot juice and give it a good shake to ensure even mixing.

Refrigerate the carrot juice for a few hours before enjoying. The juice will store in the fridge for up to 5 days. You can freeze the leftover carrot and ginger pulp for later use – try adding it to carrot cake or muffins.

NOTES

PICK FRESH CARROTS: For tastier juice, get the best carrots at your local farmers' market.

MEET MALTA: This carbonated, nonalcoholic malt beverage can be found at Hispanic or Latin American grocery stores and most bodegas. Popular brands include Goya and Vitamalt.

TIME FOR SOME SHOTS

FROM LEFT TO RIGHT:
Lemon Zinger (page 214), Apple Cider Vinegar Shot (page 214), Goji Berry Shot (page 215), Beet Shot (page 215)

Lemon Zinger

MAKES 4 (2-OUNCE/60 ML) SHOTS

If my Lemon Zinger shot doesn't show the flu who's boss, nothing will! It's like a zesty superhero punch straight to the germs.

6 unpeeled large organic lemons (see Notes)

2 unpeeled large organic oranges

2 large carrots, washed and peeled

1 (3-inch/7.5 cm) piece washed, unpeeled organic fresh ginger

2 teaspoons ground turmeric (see Notes)

¼ teaspoon cayenne pepper

Pinch of ground black pepper (see Notes)

Juice the lemons, oranges, carrots, and ginger with a juicer. Don't let the pulp go to waste; it's perfect for tea, so toss it into the freezer for when you need it. Simply add it to boiling water, let it simmer for 15 minutes, and strain.

Mix the turmeric, cayenne, and black pepper into the juice.

Pour yourself a 2-ounce (60 ml) shot. Down the hatch!

Safely store those wellness shots in an airtight jar – they'll stay fresh in the fridge for up to 4 days.

NOTES

JUICY TIP: KEEP THE PEEL! When juicing citrus, skip the peeling. Why? Citrus peels are packed with more than sixty antioxidants, bone-friendly hesperidin, and cancer-fighting d-limonene. Plus, gram for gram, they beat the fruit in vitamins and fiber. Just remember to wash your produce well, and, for a cleaner zest, opt for organic.

DYNAMIC DUO: Never leave out the black pepper when you're cooking with turmeric. It changes the game. For more on the amazing benefits of the turmeric and black pepper combo, see Notes on page 198.

Fresh or ground turmeric are both great choices.

Apple Cider Vinegar Shot

MAKES 1 (3-OUNCE/90 ML) SHOT

This shot is your wingman during fasting, workouts, and weight loss, taming those cravings like a pro. No need for a fuss—just knock back one of these! And, hey, while taking a shot of vinegar doesn't sound amazing, it's not as bad as you think. Cheers to a healthier you! Apple cider vinegar curbs cravings, eases aches, and improves your mood. Lemon juice boosts your immunity and aids digestion. Turmeric and pepper join forces to tackle inflammation. (See page 198 for more on this power couple.)

1 tablespoon apple cider vinegar

1 tablespoon fresh lemon juice

¼ teaspoon ground turmeric

⅛ teaspoon ground black pepper or cayenne

Simply mix the vinegar, lemon juice, turmeric, and pepper with 6 tablespoons (90 ml) water and serve.

Goji Berry Shot

MAKES 2 (4-OUNCE/120 ML) SHOTS

This little powerhouse packs a serious health punch. Goji berries are bursting with antioxidants, offering a robust defense against free radical damage. They're also known to enhance immune function, protect against diseases, promote healthy skin, and even boost eye health. But that's not all—these tiny fruits are also adept at stabilizing blood sugar, cleansing the liver, and improving your mood, energy, and fertility.

When paired with the zesty freshness of lemon and its abundant vitamin C, this wellness shot becomes a daily must-have. Whether you're looking to start your morning with a zest or need a midday boost, this Goji Berry Shot is your go-to for a quick sip of health and energy.

- ¾ cup (180 ml) hot water
- ¼ cup (30 g) goji berries
- 1 tablespoon fresh lemon juice

Pour the hot water over the goji berries and let them sit, covered, for 20 minutes.

Strain the berries, keeping the liquid.

Add the lemon juice to the strained goji berry liquid and serve while warm.

Beet Shot

MAKES 1 (6-OUNCE/180 ML) SHOT

This elixir is all about beets—the underrated root veggie that can boost blood flow and stamina while giving your blood pressure a friendly downward nudge. These ruby gems are the stars of the show, tackling inflammation and detoxing your system. Take this shot for a serious energy boost! This will have you stepping.

- 1 teaspoon beet powder
- Pinch of ground black pepper

Combine the beet powder and pepper with ¾ cup (180 ml) water. Drink immediately, preferably in the morning.

CRATES AND PERSONAL EFFECTS
We Provide Fast & Efficient Service
OUR NEW LOCATION AT
AVE. BETWEEN EAST 95TH AND 96TH ST. BROOKLYN, NY 11236
718.469.8377 • Fax: 718.462.1450
admin.nyc@standardshippersinc.com
LEMON
LIME
PREMIUM BANANAS
PREMIUM BANANAS
CITRICOS
Premier Citrus
Florida's Finest Oranges
Fresh From Florida

VEGAN ISLAND PANTRY

Condiments are the unsung heroes in Mauritian cuisine. But don't think of them as extras; they're costars that will steal the show. In our culinary world, small, flavorful details are essential for crafting a complete and delightful meal. And condiments are the very essence of what makes our Creole cuisine sing. They are like our ketchup and mustard. We always have jars of them in the fridge. Coconut, coriander, chili, and green mango are flavors that can transform any dish into a true tropical island extravaganza.

Any Mauritian dish I make isn't complete without the love and legacy of the incredible women in my family. I like to imagine my mum, my auntie, my grandma, and all the amazing women of Mauritius gathered around a big table to make these condiments. They're cracking open coconuts by hand, grating them with tools passed down through generations, all while swapping stories as spicy as the chiles they're slicing.

In this section, you'll learn how to make my family's most essential Mauritian condiments, spice blends that have been passed down for generations, and even my homemade coconut condensed milk.

Each dish tells a story; each chutney carries a legacy, and I'm here to guide you through creating these masterpieces, one loving spoonful at a time.

SATINI COCO
(Coconut Chutney; page 222)
PIMENT CRAZÉE
(Mauritian Chile Garlic Paste; page 221)
SATINI COTOMILI
(Cilantro Chutney; page 220)
SATINI MANGUE VERT
(Green Mango Chutney; page 223)
TAMARIND SAUCE
(page 219)
SCOTCH BONNET MANGO HOT SAUCE
(page 225)
MANGO SATINI
(Mango Chutney; page 224)

2 tablespoons tamarind paste

1 cup (240 ml) boiling water

½ tablespoon light soy sauce

1 tablespoon coconut brown sugar

1 (1-inch/2.5 cm) piece fresh ginger, peeled and thinly sliced, or ½ teaspoon ground ginger

1 dried red chile, cut into ½-inch (12 mm) pieces, or 1 teaspoon chili powder

Soak the tamarind paste in the boiling water until the pulp softens, about 5 minutes. Strain out the tamarind pulp with a fine-mesh sieve and discard it, keeping the liquid for the sauce.

In a saucepan, combine the tamarind liquid, soy sauce, sugar, ginger, and chile. Cook over medium heat until thick and syrupy, 15 to 20 minutes. Store in the fridge in a glass jar for up to 1 month.

NOTE

MAKE IT YOUR OWN: This sauce is easily adjusted to match your tastes. Add more sugar to make it sweeter. Decrease the sugar to increase tartness. Add more chile to kick up the heat. You can also add water to adjust the thickness.

Satini Cotomili (Cilantro Chutney)

MAKES 1 CUP (240 ML)

This chutney, typically paired with a savory crepe, is a symphony of flavors that hits all the right notes—it's refreshing, spicy, sweet, and salty. Brace yourself, because once you give it a try, you might find yourself tempted to slather it on everything you eat.

This versatile condiment adds a refreshing and tangy flavor to many Mauritian dishes and a pop of vibrant green color.

Try it with Gâteau Piment (Chile Cakes; page 119), Mine Frire (Mauritian Fried Noodles; page 79), Rougaille Sauce (Tomato Sauce; page 133), and more.

- ½ bunch cilantro
- 3 green chiles
- 1 clove garlic, peeled
- 1 (½-inch/12 cm) piece fresh ginger, peeled
- 1 tomato, quartered
- Salt and ground black pepper

In a blender, add the cilantro, chiles, garlic, ginger, and tomato and roughly chop.

Add ¼ cup (60 ml) water and salt and pepper to taste.

Blend everything until a smooth paste forms. Add more water as needed to reach your preferred consistency (see Note). I like it a little thick.

For the best taste, serve immediately, but you can store this chutney in a glass jar in the fridge for up to 2 months. (Remember to always use a clean spoon to serve!) If you're preparing the chutney in advance, hold off on mixing in the salt. Add it just before serving to prevent excess moisture.

Piment Crazée (Mauritian Chile Garlic Paste)

MAKES ½ CUP (120 ML)

This chile garlic paste is a beloved Mauritian condiment known for its fiery kick. It pairs perfectly with dishes that feature rougaille (pages 71, 80, and 98), Mauritian curries (pages 75 and 107), and Bol Renversé (page 72), adding depth and excitement to the dining experience. Spice enthusiasts love its intense flavor that elevates every meal it accompanies. This is an old family recipe and a permanent fixture in my fridge.

- 16 to 18 green chiles, roughly chopped
- 1 large lemon, peeled, quartered, and seeded
- 6 cloves garlic
- 2 green apples, cored and roughly chopped
- 2 medium white onions, roughly chopped
- 2 tablespoons neutral oil, plus more as needed
- 1 tablespoon salt
- 1 teaspoon brown sugar
- 1 tablespoon malt vinegar

In a small blender, add the chiles, lemon, garlic, apples, onions, oil, salt, sugar, and malt vinegar and blend into a smooth paste.

If you're enjoying the sauce right away, add a splash of water to balance out the spice. If you're storing it for future use, skip the water and mix in 4 tablespoons (60 ml) extra oil.

Store the chile paste in an airtight container in the fridge for up to 2 months.

Satini Coco (Coconut Chutney)

MAKES 1 CUP (240 ML)

When I was a kid, we would fight over this chutney! And I remember how my aunts would spend what felt like an eternity hand-grating tough coconuts to whip up jars of this stuff for the whole family. They were kitchen warriors—the dedication was real!

When I'm creating this masterpiece, fresh grated coconut adds a delightful touch, but I usually opt for store-bought grated coconut for convenience. Satini Coco pairs beautifully with a variety of dishes, including curries, lentil crepes (page 92), and even salads, adding a tropical and savory element that elevates the flavors.

- 1½ cups (150 g) grated fresh coconut
- 1 tablespoon tamarind paste
- Salt
- 3 to 5 small green chiles, roughly chopped
- ½ cup (25 g) mint leaves
- 2 cloves garlic
- 1 tablespoon avocado oil
- ½ teaspoon mustard seeds
- ½ teaspoon urad dal (black lentils)
- 2 dried red chiles, such as Thai bird's eye, broken in half
- 10 fresh curry leaves

In a blender, add the coconut, tamarind paste, salt, green chiles, mint, and garlic. Blend into a fine paste. You may have to add a splash of water to obtain a paste-like consistency. Transfer the chutney to a large bowl.

In a cast-iron pan over high heat, heat the oil to prepare for tempering (see page 20 for more on this technique). When the oil is hot, add one mustard seed: when it sizzles, the oil is ready. Add the remaining mustard seeds and let them start to pop, then add the urad dal and red chiles. Sauté for 30 seconds or until the dal starts turning green. Add the curry leaves, stir, and remove the pan from the heat.

Pour the contents of the pan, including the oil, over the bowl of chutney, stir, and serve. Store the chutney in an airtight container in the fridge for up to 2 months.

Satini Mangue Vert (Green Mango Chutney)

MAKES 1 CUP (240 ML)

In my mom's backyard in Mauritius, there stood a mango tree. One sunny day, my mom and her siblings decided it was time for a mango raid. With buckets in hand and mischief in their eyes, they plucked a few green mangoes from the branches, feeling like fruit bandits on a delicious mission. They got in trouble, but not before enjoying a feast—which was well worth it.

I have my own childhood memories of mangoes. The aunts would gather on the veranda, set up an outdoor kitchen, and start grating the golden-green treasures to make mango chutney. It was a fruit production line, with everyone playing their part. For the grand finale, we'd receive a mango seed, a sweet reward for our fruity conquest. Sucking on that seed was our victory lap, a celebration of a successful mission.

This pairs perfectly with Jerk Mushroom Tacos (page 83), Green Curry with Tofu Fish, Eggplant, and Rice Cakes (page 75), and No Shrimp Curry (page 107).

- 2 green (unripe) mangoes
- 1 teaspoon salt, plus more as needed
- 1 teaspoon ground turmeric
- 2 tablespoons rice vinegar
- 3 tablespoons neutral oil
- 1 teaspoon black mustard seeds, roughly crushed
- 1 small white onion, thinly sliced
- 2 green chiles, thinly sliced
- 3 teaspoons store-bought garlic paste
- 3 teaspoons grated fresh ginger

Peel and grate the mangoes into a bowl. Salt the mangoes and let them sit for around 10 minutes, then squeeze the mango, discarding the liquid.

In a small bowl, combine the turmeric and vinegar.

In a cast-iron pan over high heat, heat the oil to prepare for tempering. When the oil is hot, add one mustard seed: when it sizzles, the oil is ready. Add the remaining mustard seeds and let them start to pop, then add the onion, chiles, garlic paste, and grated ginger and cook until the onion is brown.

Add the turmeric-vinegar mixture, stirring to combine and scraping up any browned bits, then add the mangoes and stir well. Add salt to taste.

Turn off the heat and leave the chutney to cool. Store it in a glass jar in the fridge for up to 2 months.

Mango Satini (Mango Chutney)

MAKES ¼ CUP (120 ML)

In the heart of Mauritius, where the air is filled with the scent of spices and the ocean's breeze, there lies a kitchen treasure that captures the island's spirit: mango satini. This chutney is more than just a condiment; it's a celebration of our local produce and a testament to our rich cultural tapestry.

Made from the freshest green mangoes, each bite of mango satini is a perfect blend of tangy, sweet, and spicy flavors. The mangoes are picked at just the right time to ensure they carry that perfect punch of sourness, which contrasts beautifully with the heat from the chiles and the subtle complexity of garlic and other spices. In comparison to other mango chutneys, this chutney is not as sweet, but more tangy, and bursting with spices. It's not merely a side dish but a crucial component that brings life to every meal, be it alongside curries, grilled meats, or simply spread over a warm piece of roti.

This recipe I'm about to share has been passed down through generations, tweaked slightly with each passing hand, but always retaining the essence of Mauritian hospitality and warmth. Whether you're a seasoned chef or a curious foodie, making Mango Satini will bring a taste of Mauritius right into your kitchen. So, let's embark on this flavorful journey together, where each step is a dance of colors and each spoonful a celebration of our island's vibrant palette.

- 2 green (unripe) large mangoes
- 2 tablespoons unrefined coconut oil
- 2 teaspoons red pepper flakes
- 1 teaspoon black mustard seeds
- Juice of 3 lemons
- Salt

Peel and grate the mangoes.

In a medium frying pan, heat the oil over medium-high heat. Add the mangoes, red pepper flakes, mustard seeds, and lemon juice. Stir well until the mixture starts to caramelize, about 10 minutes. Add salt to taste.

Leave the chutney to cool. Store it in a glass jar in the fridge for up to 1 week.

Scotch Bonnet Mango Hot Sauce

MAKES 1 (16-OUNCE/480 ML) JAR

This fiery sauce combines the heat of Scotch bonnet peppers with the tropical sweetness of mangoes.

In my kitchen, this unique hot sauce is a staple condiment, adding a kick of heat and a touch of sweetness to a wide range of dishes. It pairs exceptionally well with my ackee (page 42), fried dumplings (page 44), avocado toast (page 62), and plantain waffle (page 47).

- 1 large mango, peeled and diced
- 1 carrot, peeled and roughly chopped
- 1 yellow bell pepper, roughly chopped
- 1 medium red onion, roughly chopped
- 4 cloves garlic
- 2 scallions
- 8 Scotch bonnet peppers, stalks removed and deseeded
- 1 teaspoon pink salt
- 2 tablespoons coconut sugar
- Juice of 2 limes
- 2 teaspoons ground ginger
- 1 teaspoon ground cumin

In a blender or food processor, add the mango, carrot, bell pepper, red onion, garlic, scallions, and Scotch bonnets. Puree, adding water as needed, until it is a pouring consistency, like barbeque sauce.

Transfer the puree to a skillet over high heat and heat until it starts to splutter, then reduce the heat to low. Add the pink salt, coconut sugar, lime juice, ginger, and cumin. Cover and simmer for 20 minutes, stirring often. Add a splash of water if it starts to stick.

Let the mixture cool, then return it to the blender and puree until smooth. Make sure the mixture is completely cool before blending to avoid getting splashed with hot liquid.

Transfer the sauce to an airtight container and refrigerate. This sauce can be stored in the fridge for up to 6 months.

Creamy Cashew-Based Tzatziki

MAKES 1 CUP (240 ML)

Cashews and crunchy cucumber are the perfect duo for making an amazing vegan tzatziki. With its creamy texture and refreshing taste, this plant-based delight is a game-changer, whether you're using it as a dip, a spread, or a sauce. Try it as a dip with fresh veggies, soft pita, or pita chips, or a sauce with my East London Kebab Shop Gyro (page 108).

1½ cups (180 g) raw cashews

Boiled water

½ cup (120 ml) lemon juice, plus more as needed

2 tablespoons distilled white vinegar

2 large cloves garlic, minced

¾ teaspoon salt, plus more as needed

¼ teaspoon ground black pepper, plus more as needed

1 large cucumber, peeled and grated

¼ cup (13 g) chopped fresh dill

Place the cashews in a heatproof bowl. Pour enough boiled water to cover the cashews. Let them soak for 15 to 20 minutes, until they feel soft when squeezed between your fingertips, then drain.

In a blender or food processor, add ¾ cup (180 ml) water and the soaked cashews, lemon juice, vinegar, garlic, salt, and pepper. Blend the mixture on high speed until it achieves a smooth and creamy consistency.

Add the cucumber and dill to the blender. Pulse the blender a few times to combine. (Alternatively, for a sauce with more texture, transfer the sauce base to a bowl and stir in the cucumber and dill by hand.)

Taste the sauce and adjust the seasoning, if necessary, adding extra salt, pepper, or lemon juice according to your preference.

Chill the sauce in a covered container in the refrigerator until you're ready to serve. It can be stored in an airtight container in the refrigerator for up to 2 days.

Kebab Shop Chili Sauce

MAKES 1 CUP (240 ML)

This recipe whisks me back to electrifying nights in East London kebab shops, where the real hero was the fiery chili sauce. The thrill, the taste, and the unmistakable aroma that lingered in the air—I wanted to capture it all.

Elsewhere in my cookbook, you can re-create the sizzle of the grill (see my East London Kebab Shop Gyro, page 108), but for now let's focus on the signature sauce that made those nights so special.

I've crafted a vegan version of that zesty, garlicky delight. And the best part? It's perfect for everyone! Whether you're a seasoned spice pro, daring your taste buds to the max, or just dipping your toes into the world of heat, you can tailor this sauce to you. Let's bring some of that unforgettable kebab shop magic to your kitchen!

- ¼ cup (60 ml) olive oil
- ½ teaspoon salt
- 1 (14-ounce/400 g) can chopped tomatoes
- 2 tablespoons tomato puree
- 1 small yellow or white onion, peeled and roughly chopped
- 4 cloves garlic, peeled
- 3 or 4 red chiles, roughly chopped, seeds and all (see Note)
- 1 tablespoon distilled white vinegar or apple cider vinegar

To a mini chopper or food processor, add the olive oil, salt, tomatoes, tomato puree, onion, garlic, chiles, and vinegar and blitz to make a sauce.

Pour the sauce into a saucepan over medium heat and bring to a gentle simmer. Cook for 5 to 10 minutes or until you reach a thick consistency.

The sauce will keep in an airtight container in the fridge for up to 2 days or in the freezer for up to 3 months.

NOTE

CHOOSING CHILES: For a medium-hot kick, I recommend fresh red Thai (bird's-eye) chiles. If you're not a fan of heat, use a mild pepper like serrano. Or, if you're craving even more heat, opt for Scotch bonnet or habanero chiles. If you dare, elevate the spice level with ghost chiles or Carolina Reapers for a wildly hot sauce.

Homemade Coconut Condensed Milk

MAKES 1 (16-OUNCE/480 ML) JAR

Condensed milk is a staple in any Jamaican household. You can use it in many desserts, including puddings, ice creams, cakes, and fudge, as well as caramel sauce and candy. Add a dollop to your porridge for a sweet and creamy twist, or stir a spoonful into your tea, coffee, or hot cocoa. You can even add some to cold beverages for a velvety touch.

1 (13½-ounce/400 ml) can unsweetened coconut milk

¼ cup (50 g) coconut brown sugar

In a saucepan, bring the coconut milk to a boil over high heat. Watch it closely to prevent burning or bubbling over.

Reduce the heat to low, then whisk in the coconut sugar thoroughly. Let the mixture simmer for 40 to 45 minutes, stirring occasionally. After about 20 minutes, the mixture will thicken slightly and take on a dark brown hue. Its consistency should be similar to caramel.

Once you achieve your desired texture, set it aside to cool to room temperature. Transfer the mixture to a jar and refrigerate until completely chilled. The mixture will thicken fully as it chills.

The sweetened condensed milk lasts for roughly 1 week stored in an airtight jar in the fridge.

Jerk Dry Rub Seasoning

MAKES ¼ CUP (30 G)

Bring the bold and vibrant flavors of Jamaica to your table with my jerk dry rub. This flavorful gem adds that extra kick to a variety of dishes, from roasted vegetables to salad dressings and even mayonnaise!

The history of jerk spice is deeply intertwined with the cultural heritage of Jamaica, tracing its roots back to the Maroons, who were descendants of West African slaves who escaped from plantations and sought refuge in the rugged mountains of Jamaica. They would marinate meat in a spice blend before slow-cooking it over a wood fire until it was succulent and flavorful. The term "jerk" is believed to have originated from the Spanish word "charqui," meaning dried or preserved meat.

Jerk spice is a distinctive and aromatic blend of ingredients that were readily available in Jamaica, including allspice (also known as pimento), thyme, garlic, onions, cinnamon, nutmeg, and cloves. Over time, it has become an integral part of Jamaican cuisine and culture.

I use this homemade jerk spice for marinating and seasoning vegetables and tofu, in salad dressings, and even to dress up mayonnaise!

- 1 tablespoon onion powder
- 1 tablespoon garlic powder
- 2 teaspoons cayenne pepper
- 2 teaspoons ground black pepper
- 2 teaspoons dried thyme
- 2 teaspoons coconut brown sugar
- 1 teaspoon ground allspice
- 1 teaspoon dried parsley
- 1 teaspoon smoked paprika
- ½ teaspoon red pepper flakes
- ½ teaspoon ground cinnamon
- ½ teaspoon ground nutmeg
- ½ teaspoon ground cloves
- ¼ teaspoon ground cumin

Using a spoon or whisk, thoroughly mix the onion powder, garlic powder, cayenne, black pepper, thyme, brown sugar, allspice, parsley, paprika, red pepper flakes, cinnamon, nutmeg, cloves, and cumin until well combined. Make sure there are no clumps or uneven pockets of seasoning – you want a homogeneous blend.

Store the seasoning in a tightly sealed jar or other airtight container at room temperature for up to 6 months.

CLOCKWISE FROM TOP:
Eggy Seasoning Mix (page 232), All-Purpose Seasoning (page 233), Homemade Mauritian Curry Powder (page 231), Jerk Dry Rub Seasoning (page 229)

Homemade Mauritian Curry Powder

MAKES ¾ CUP (80 G)

This homemade curry powder recipe, passed down from my aunts, is the secret to adding an authentic Mauritian touch to your dishes! While store-bought options are convenient, there's something truly special about crafting your own blend of spices. Not only does it offer a subtle yet distinctive twist to traditional Indian curry powders, but it also allows you to tailor the flavors to your liking. With just a few simple steps, you can create a spice mix that brings the unique essence of Mauritian cuisine to your kitchen, elevating your dishes with depth and complexity.

6 tablespoons (30 g) coriander seeds

2½ tablespoons cumin seeds

4 teaspoons fennel seeds

1 tablespoon fenugreek seeds

1 (1-inch/2.5 cm) piece cinnamon stick

4 whole dried red chiles, broken into pieces (discard most of the seeds)

5 dried curry leaves

4 teaspoons ground turmeric

EQUIPMENT:

Spice grinder or clean coffee grinder

Heat a medium pan, preferably cast iron, on low to medium heat. Ensure the heat is not too high, to prevent the spices from scorching.

Once the pan is hot, add the coriander seeds, cumin seeds, fennel seeds, fenugreek seeds, and cinnamon stick. Gently stir until aromatic, about 1 minute.

Add the chiles and curry leaves. Continue to stir gently for 1 or 2 more minutes, until you can smell the delightful fragrance of the curry leaves.

Add the turmeric and give the mixture a quick stir. Immediately remove the pan from the heat and allow the spice mix to cool completely.

Once the spices are cool, use a spice grinder to grind them into a fine powder.

Transfer the ground curry powder to an airtight container, preferably glass, and store it in a cool, dark place. This homemade blend keeps for several months.

Eggy Seasoning Mix

MAKES 2 CUPS (200 G)

This vegan blend is carefully crafted to capture the essence of eggs. Each component plays a crucial role in replicating eggs' distinctive taste and color.

Firstly, kala namak, or Himalayan black salt. This isn't your average table salt—it's the secret ingredient that brings that unmistakable eggy essence to vegan dishes with its sulfurous tang. Whether you're a longtime vegan missing that eggy flavor or just adventurous with your palate, black salt is something you'll want to keep within arm's reach in your kitchen. You can easily find it at any Indian food store or with a quick online search, often at a steal. It's one of those culinary treasures that, once you know about, you can't help but share with others!

Next up is nutritional yeast, a powerhouse ingredient known for being rich in umami. Not only does it enhance the savory notes of our blend, but it also adds a layer of complexity that mimics the depth of flavor found in eggs.

Turmeric, with its earthy and slightly smoky undertones, not only lends a vibrant yellow hue to our mixture but also imparts a subtle hint of smokiness reminiscent of cooked eggs. Onion and garlic powder round out the flavor profile, adding a touch of sweetness and earthiness.

Together, these ingredients work in perfect synergy to create a plant-based egg flavoring that's not only delicious but also versatile enough to elevate a wide range of dishes. Whether you're making scrambled "eggs," vegan omelets, or incorporating it into your favorite recipes, this blend promises to deliver the unmistakable essence of eggs without compromising on your dietary preferences.

- 2 cups (120 g) nutritional yeast
- 14 teaspoons (84 g) Himalayan black salt
- 10 teaspoons (20 g) onion powder
- 4 teaspoons garlic powder
- 4 teaspoons turmeric

In a sealable jar, combine the nutritional yeast, black salt, onion powder, garlic powder, and turmeric and shake well or stir to combine. Store in the pantry until ready to use, or up to 6 months.

All-Purpose Seasoning

MAKES ⅓ CUP (30 G)

Introducing my secret weapon for flavor-packed dishes: my homemade all-purpose seasoning blend! This is a staple in every Jamaican household. With a medley of herbs like aromatic oregano, bitter celery seeds, and earthy thyme, this seasoning is a game-changer for elevating the taste of your savory creations. Garlic powder brings a savory element, while onion powder adds a touch of sweetness. Pepper gives it heat and boldness, and paprika introduces some vibrant color and smokiness. Finally, salt balances all the flavors! This spice blend is quick to make, requiring just five minutes and ten pantry staples. It will transform soups, stews, salads, marinades, barbecue . . . the list is endless. Say goodbye to bland meals and hello to effortless gourmet flavor!

2 tablespoons garlic powder

2 tablespoons onion powder

1 tablespoon ground black pepper

1 tablespoon paprika

2 teaspoons dried thyme

2 teaspoons dried oregano

2 teaspoons celery seeds

1 tablespoon salt (optional)

In a clean bowl or jar, combine the garlic powder, onion powder, pepper, paprika, thyme, oregano, celery seeds, and salt, if using. Keep the seasoning mix in an airtight container in your pantry for up to 3 months.

KEEP PUSHING AGAINST THE FLOW

(My father's words throughout my childhood, and they've always reminded me to stay strong and keep moving forward, no matter what.)

This cookbook emerged from a place of profound loss and transformation. Losing my hero, my father, Whylie Rookwood, marked the beginning of my journey toward wellness and self-discovery. When he was diagnosed with stage 4 stomach cancer, I fought tirelessly to save him holistically. That battle changed me forever. My father passed away on New Year's Day 2011, at the stroke of midnight—a moment so characteristic of his spirit—going out with a bang and a celebration, just as he lived his life.

The journey through his illness opened my eyes to the profound connection between food and well-being, igniting my path to a plant-based lifestyle. I now see my father's passing as both a gift and a blessing. His legacy lives on in every choice I make and every meal I prepare. He gave me a second chance to live fully and healthily, a gift that extends to his granddaughter, Emi, whom he never had the chance to meet.

We are living testaments to his influence, embodying resilience and strength born from pain and sacrifice. As we keep pushing against the flow, we honor his memory and the wisdom he imparted. This book is a heartfelt tribute to my father's enduring spirit, his love for Yahweh, and the love he instilled in me for nourishing our bodies and souls.

Acknowledgments

Creating this cookbook has been a journey of passion, creativity, and community. It's a project that flourished not just from culinary experiments, but from the incredible support and inspiration I received along the way. I am profoundly grateful to everyone who contributed to, supported, and guided me through this adventure. Every page reflects the enthusiasm and dedication of a group of remarkable individuals.

First, I want to express my deepest appreciation to Kate Spade New York for adding an element of sophistication and style to my cookbook. Your products bring beauty into every kitchen, and having your support has been a dream come true. A special thank-you goes out to Iris Coker: your encouragement and positivity have been a beacon for me.

To Drew Barrymore and your beautiful brand of cookware, thank you for making our culinary creations look as good as they taste. Your involvement has added a sparkle that perfectly complements the flavors within these pages.

Shae Hong, thank you for the hookups and the endless support. Your generosity has been a cornerstone of this project's success.

Shabnam, my sis, you've connected me with so many incredible plant-based brands that I've featured throughout this book. I am so grateful for you always giving me the inside scoop before things even hit the shops. You're like my own little vegan product secret agent!

A huge thank you to Chef Chris Tucker—you made sure that Yo Egg got to me from LA overnight like magic. You are truly a legend.

It really does take a village, and I'm thankful for each and every one of you!

A heartfelt thanks to Victoria Akkari, whose handmade ceramic gems have transformed my dishes into art. Each piece you've contributed is not just a tool but a treasure. Your choice to not follow trends has led us to beautiful pieces sourced from extraordinarily talented women. Your vision truly sets us apart.

Maria, you connected the dots—thank you for being my rock, love ya.

Mandy! What a year it's been . . . all those late-night conversations about life, me venting about trying to land a cookbook deal while navigating this roller-coaster called life. I couldn't have done it without you by my side, reminding me to stay grounded and keep pushing through it all.

Necklace credit: Selly Raby Kane.

Dinosaur Designs Australian Design Studio, I've never seen resin-based home decor like yours. Absolutely breathtaking.

Special gratitude goes to my family and the members of our three musketeers, Ken and Emi, my biggest supporters. Your love and encouragement mean the world to me – love you both to the moon and back.

My mum, the heart and soul behind so much of who I am. Your unwavering support, endless patience, and the warmth of your Creole Mauritian roots have shaped this cookbook into something truly special. Every recipe carries the essence of your love and the vibrant flavors you've passed down to me. Thank you for being my best friend, my confidant, and my greatest believer. I hope the world can handle the heat you've blessed me with.

To my daughter, Emi, you are my sunshine and constant source of joy. Your boundless creativity and vibrant spirit inspire me every day. I hope this book reminds you that anything is possible when you follow your heart. You made my life complete.

Having Emi on set with her grandma Shizuko meant the world to me. Three generations of female empowerment cooking together, merging influences from Jamaica, Mauritius, Japan, and Austria, was truly special. Thank you for adding the Augarten porcelain to the cookbook. What an honor to include such fine tableware with a three-hundred-year tradition all the way from Vienna.

Edgar, even though you're not here with us physically, your spirit comes alive every time I make your goulash. I can feel the echoes of your laughter, the humor of your jokes, and the warmth of your smile. This dish is a living legacy, bridging the gaps of time and space. As I pass down your recipe to your granddaughter Emi, I'm honoring your long heritage of love, connection, and enduring joy. It's my way of keeping you close and sharing the traditions that mean so much to our family. I know you are now reunited with Kiki, your partner in crime. And that warms my heart.

Many hands and hearts touched this cookbook behind the scenes. I was blessed with the most amazing crew on set.

Clay Williams, thank you for being open to my Vegan Soulicious vision and for capturing my story, ancestors, and flavor through your camera lens. It was such an honor to work with you.

Luciana Lamboy, food stylist and recipe developer, you made the magic happen on every plate, styled to perfection. Thank you for guiding me through the process with lots of laughter and singing.

Sarah French, my right hand in the kitchen, thank you for holding me down and always staying ten steps ahead. Let's see what the universe throws at us next.

Mother-and-daughter-duo extraordinaire Gerri K. Williams, prop stylist/art director, and Sadie Frost, prop stylist assistant, I don't know where to start! I was so spoiled with the number of props on set – sorry, correction, a U-Haul truck of props! The energy and positivity you brought on set were essential.

Devin Armstrong, assistant photographer, you clearly came to also be the food tester and BTS secret snapper who brought good vibes every day.

Trevis L. Lester, you know no one else can do my makeup but you! It's like a karaoke session while the transformation takes place. Thank you for always being by my side and making me feel fabulous.

Patricia Moote, you didn't just do my hair – you turned into a Home Depot runner and saved the day. You are a real one. Thank you, sis!

Daniel Williams, stylist, you pulled up and we shut New York City down with this lifestyle shoot! Good vibrations always, appreciate you, brother.

Paris and Anthony, owners of Soft & Well, thank you for taming these curly locks and bringing back the bounce.

Ronna Welsh at Purple Kale Kitchenworks, you blessed me with the perfect space to shoot my cookbook, and I will be eternally grateful.

My dear Angie Vasquez, each photo tells a story, and that's all thanks to you. Your ability to capture the candid moments – the laughter in my eyes and the joy that food brings into my life – elevates this book from mere instruction to an intimate portrait of my culinary journey. Your photography has not only documented my journey for the past five years, it has become a part of it. Thank you for seeing me, not just as I cook, but as I am. I am so grateful for your friendship and your incredible gift.

I want to thank my sister from another mista, Dahlia. You've been by my side through every twist and turn, forever holding me down and showing me what true friendship is. Thank you for being my longest, most loyal friend.

To Tanya Moore, my sister in spirit and vision, your belief in me sparked a journey I could only dream of. You saw potential where I only saw a glimmer and gave me the chance to launch *The Black Vegan Cooking Show* – a gift that has transformed my life in ways I never imagined. Your support, love, and faith in me have led to the creation of this cookbook, and for that, I am endlessly grateful. You always knew I could do it, and here we are, shining together. Black girls rock, and so does our shared dream. Thank you for being the driving force behind this incredible journey.

Christopher Williams, thank you for your spiritual guidance. Your wisdom and support have been a beacon of light throughout this journey. May Yahweh continue to bless us both abundantly.

Amie Parnes, without you none of this would have been possible. Thank you for introducing me to Bridget Matzie. The rest is history!

Bridget Wagner Matzie, you believed in me from the jump and understood my mission, purpose, and passion to make this cookbook. You are far more than my literary agent; you are now a part of my sister circle. I appreciate you more than words can say. This is just the beginning of our adventure!

Elena Steiert, you came to the rescue and made sense of my words and turned it into a cookbook! You are the most patient human I know!

Laura Dozier, thank you for taking a leap of faith and making one of my dreams come true. I know I'm a little unconventional with my approach to everything, but that's the Vegan Soulicious vibe. Thank you for your patience and understanding.

Diane Shaw, thank you for your guidance and creative eye. You just get me, and that means a lot. You have a way of calming me down when needed.

I'd like to extend a heartfelt thank you to Annie Marino for her incredible talent and attention to detail in designing the layout of these pages, bringing them to life so beautifully.

To Towel Boy – you have the eye of the tiger and see art in ways like no other! Thank you for adding the final touches and finesse. I could not have done this without you.

REST IN POWER, AUNTIE DOR AND MY DAD

DADDY'S GIRL

MY PARENTS ARE THE COOLEST.

EDGAR — "OPA."
THE MASTERMIND
BEHIND THE GOULASH.

BERNICE & FERDINAND

MY DAD CLIMBED THAT TREE IN JAMAICA TO GET US THOSE COCONUTS!

GRAND-MÉRE—
"ONE FOR YOU, ONE FOR ME."

LAST PHOTO OF DAD

MY DAD WAS SUPER FLY!

Plant-Based Online Shopping Recommendations

When it comes to sourcing the best ingredients for your plant-based recipes, convenience and quality are key. These online shopping options cater to different needs and preferences within the vegan community, ensuring that you have access to a wide array of plant-based products no matter where you are. Happy cooking and happy shopping!

VEGAN ESSENTIALS

The longest-operating cruelty-free retailer in the United States, this business has been vegan owned and operated since 1997.

veganessentials.com

IHEARTFRUITBOX

Enjoy tropical seasonal and seeded fruit shipped straight to your door anywhere in the continental US and Canada from an amazing Black-owned farm!

iheartfruitbox.com

IMPERFECT FOODS

Reduce food waste and save money with Imperfect Foods. They deliver "imperfect" produce – vegetables and fruit that would not have made it to the shelves because they are not perfectly shaped – and surplus groceries at discounted prices, including a variety of vegan options.

imperfectfoods.com

THE VEGAN KIND MARKET

If you are looking for a UK-based option, Vegan Kind is your answer. Their curated collection of vegan groceries, including pantry staples and ethical household products, is sure to impress.

vegankind.com

THRIVE MARKET

With a focus on organic, non-GMO, and vegan products, Thrive Market is a go-to for stocking up on pantry staples, snacks, supplements, and eco-friendly household items. Their discounts make it even more appealing for budget-conscious shoppers, but you do need to pay for a membership to access the savings.

thrivemarket.com

TROPICAL FRUIT BOX

This is another convenient source for tropical and exotic fruits.

tropicalfruitbox.com

VEGAN ESSENTIALS

As its name suggests, Vegan Essentials is a paradise for all things vegan. From plant-based foods to cruelty-free beauty products and even vegan clothing, they have a vast selection that caters to every aspect of a vegan lifestyle.

veganessentials.com

VITACOST

While not exclusively vegan, Vitacost boasts a wide range of vegan-friendly products across food, supplements, beauty, and household categories. Keep an eye out for their discounts and promotions on vegan brands.

vitacost.com

PLANTAINS
Dole
BANANAS
Patrona
CHULA
Kapi
Dole
Chiquita

Celebrating Community

Nothing beats shopping local and giving back to the community. As an islander, I always source the produce I need daily from Caribbean and Indian stores. My go-to is Labay Market in Brooklyn, delivering farm-to-table produce straight from Grenada. Big shoutout to the owner, Big Mac, for blessing my cookbook with the most amazing produce! Thank you for all you do for the community. You are an icon!

Supporting Black-owned local businesses is not just a choice for me; it's a passion and a celebration of our culture. The fresh, vibrant produce from Labay Market embodies the spirit and resilience of our community. They provide quality products and enrich our cultural heritage, making every purchase a step toward empowering our own. Let's continue to uplift and support our Black entrepreneurs—our community's heart and soul.

More Than an Apron

My Vegan Soulicious aprons and headwraps have not only been essential in my kitchen but have also beautifully graced the pages of this book as vibrant backdrops. This project is a collaboration with The Dennis Sharpe Foundation, a charity that holds a special place in my heart.

Focused on the town of Kasoa, in the Central Region of Ghana, the foundation is empowering local women by developing their skills and expanding their opportunities beyond just small alterations and local crafts.

Opting for Ghana over a team in the USA was a personal choice, deeply rooted in my family's history. My late father's business ventures in Accra left me with wonderful memories, and setting foot in Ghana always feels like returning home.

Having my sisters join me in this project has been extraordinarily meaningful. Our collective goal is to help these skilled women gain access to international markets, including the USA, UK, and Europe, fostering their ability to support themselves through their craftsmanship.

Financial aid is just the beginning. Real empowerment comes from consistent action, creative thinking, and robust global connections. Our commitment is to empower these individuals profoundly, ensuring we make a lasting impact on marginalized communities.

The mission statement of The Dennis Sharpe Foundation is straightforward: "To educate, empower, and mobilize future generations one step at a time."

The success of this project is a testament to the power of good people coming together.

A heartfelt thanks to Eldridge Cooke – you truly were the glue that brought this project together. Thank you for your unwavering commitment and spirit. You know my father is loving the slicker "Whylie Moves" you are making!

As we continue our efforts, we are reminded that every small push against the current nurtures growth and brings us closer to our goals.

Index

A

Ackee and "No Saltfish"
- Plantain Breakfast Waffle, 46, 47
- recipe, 42–43

All-Purpose Seasoning, 230, *230*, 233

allspice, 22, *22*, 23
- Jamaican Sorrel, *188–89*, 189, *192*, 193
- Jerk Dry Rub Seasoning, 229, 230, *230*
- Jerk Mushroom Tacos, *82*, 83

almond milk, 48, *49*

apple
- Piment Crazée, 218, *218*, 221
- Sweet Potato Juice, *204*, 205, 206
- Ugo Verde, 205, *205*, 210

Apple Cider Vinegar Shot, *212*, 213, 214

artichoke hearts
- Jamaican "No Saltfish" Fritters, 36, *37*, 38, *39*

atta flour
- Effortless Homemade Chapatis, *152*, 153

avocado, 18, *18*
- Jamaican Avocado Toast with Fried Plantains, 62, *63*
- Plantain Breakfast Waffle, *46*, 47

B

bacon, vegan, 28
- Jamaican Cabbage and Bacon, 142, *143*
- Super Fluffy "Bacon" Pancakes, *54*, 55, *56–57*, 57

banana blossoms
- Vegan Fish and Chips, *94*, 95–96, *97*

bananas. *See also* green bananas; plantain
- Breakfast Cereal Sea Moss Shake, 48, *49*
- Cacao, Sea Moss, and Maca Smoothie Bowl, *50*, 51
- Coconut Banana Fritters, 160, *160–61*, *172*, 173
- Super Fluffy "Bacon" Pancakes, *54*, 55, *56–57*, 57
- Tropical Charcoal Detox Smoothie Bowl, 52, *53*

basil
- Creole Rum Passion Cocktail, *188*, 189, 191
- seeds, *184*, 185
- Thai, 18, *18*

beans. *See also* green beans
- Haricots Rouges (Spiced Red Kidney Beans) and Rice, 146, *147*
- Mauritian Butter Bean Soup, 101, 102, *102*

beef, vegan
- East London Kebab Shop Gyro, 108, *109*
- Jamaican Vegan Beef Puffs, 122, *123*

beer
- Jamaican Guinness Punch, *188*, 189, 190

Beet Shot, 213, *213*, 215

bell pepper
- Bol Renversé, 72, *73*, 74, *74*
- Green Banana Rundown, 84, *85*
- Jamaican Cabbage and Bacon, 142, *143*
- Jamaican "No Saltfish" Fritters, 36, *37*, 38, *39*
- Mine Frire, *78*, 79
- Scotch Bonnet Mango Hot Sauce, 218, *218*, 225
- Vegetable Achard, *136*, 137

bitter gourd
- Margose Frire (Stir-Fried Bitter Gourd), 156, *157*, 160, *160*

black pepper
- All-Purpose Seasoning, 230, *230*, 233
- turmeric and, benefits of, 198

Black Vegan Cooking Show, The, 11, 108, 159, 166

blood orange
- Galangal Blood Orange Tea, *196*, 197, 198

blueberries
- Tropical Charcoal Detox Smoothie Bowl, 52, *53*

bok choy
- Mine Frire, *78*, 79

Bol Renversé (Magic Bowl), 72, *73*, 74, *74*

Bouillon Cresson (Watercress Broth) with Crispy Lion's Mane Mushrooms, 98, *99*

bread (as ingredient)
- Brioche Bread Pudding, *164*, 165
- Chile and Makrut Lime Garlic Bread, 158, 160, *160*
- East London Kebab Shop Gyro, 108, *109*
- Edgar's Vegan Goulash, *110*, 111
- Jamaican Avocado Toast with Fried Plantains, 62, *63*
- Mauritian Gâteau Arouille, *114–15*, 120, *121*
- Tropical Plantain and "Egg" Breakfast Sandwiches, 66, *67*

breadfruit
- Roasted and Fried Breadfruit Wedges, 126, *127*

Breakfast Cereal Sea Moss Shake, 48, *49*

Brioche Bread Pudding, *164*, 165

brown sugar. *See* coconut sugar

butter, vegan, 28

C

cabbage
- Coleslaw, *82*, 83
- Jamaican Cabbage and Bacon, 142, *143*
- Lisou Touffé (Mauritian Sautéed Cabbage), 140
- Mine Frire, *78*, 79
- One-Pot Pumpkin Soup, 102, *102*, 103
- Vegetable Achard, *136*, 137

cacao
- Cacao, Sea Moss, and Maca Smoothie Bowl, *50*, 51
- Jamaican Chocolate Tea, 197, *197*, 201

cactus, 18, *18*
- Ugo Verde, 205, *205*, 210

Cajun seasoning, 84, *85*

Callaloo Sauté, *45*, 141

cancer, 15, 198, 206, 214, 235

capers, 95–96

cardamom, 19, 22, *22*
- Coconut Brown Sugar Rice Pudding, *64*, 65
- Gâteaux Koko, *176*, 177
- Pilau Rice, *148*, 149

carrot
- Bol Renversé, 72, *73*, 74, *74*
- Carrot Juice, 205, *205*, 211
- Coleslaw, *82*, 83
- Fricasser Lentilles Noires, *138*, 139
- Jamaican Cabbage and Bacon, 142, *143*
- Lemon Zinger, *212*, 213, 214
- Mine Frire, *78*, 79

One-Pot Pumpkin Soup, 102, *102*, 103
Scotch Bonnet Mango Hot Sauce, 218, *218*, 225
Vegetable Achard, *136*, 137
cashews
The Creamiest, Cheesiest Vegan Mac 'n' Cheese – Ever!, 159, 160, *161*
Creamy Cashew-Based Tzatziki, 108, 226
cast-iron pan, 29
Cavi-art products, 27, 107
cayenne, 155, 194, 202, 214
Jerk Dry Rub Seasoning, 229, 230, *230*
celery salt, 90, 95, 98
celery seeds
All-Purpose Seasoning, 230, *230*, 233
charcoal powder
Tropical Charcoal Detox Smoothie Bowl, 52, *53*
cheese, vegan, 28
The Creamiest, Cheesiest Vegan Mac 'n' Cheese – Ever!, 159, 160, *161*
chia seeds, 51, 52, 165, 185
chicken-flavored seasoning
Vegan Fried Chicken, 88, *89*, 90, *91*
chickpea flour
Crispy Onion Bhajis, *114–15*, 116, *117*
children, 15–16
chiles, 19. *See also* green chiles; Scotch bonnet peppers
Chile and Makrut Lime Garlic Bread, 158, 160, *160*
Fricasser Lentilles Noires, *138*, 139
Homemade Mauritian Curry Powder, 230, *230*, 231
Kebab Shop Chili Sauce, 108, 227
Lisou Touffé, 140
Mango Chile Lassi, *60*, 61
Margose Frire, 156, *157*, 160, *160*
Mauritian Cucumber Salad, *144*, 145
Satini Coco, 218, *218*, 222
Tamarind Sauce, 218, *218*, 219
Tofu Vindaye, *86*, 87
Touffer Haricots Verts à la Mauricienne, 100, 102, *102*
Chili Salt, 170, *171*
chocolate. *See also* cacao
Date Candy Bar, 166, *167–69*
Jamaican Chocolate Tea, 197, *197*, 201
cilantro, 19, 92, *93*, 102, *102*
Chile and Makrut Lime Garlic Bread, 158, 160, *160*
Gâteau Piment, *114–15*, *118*, 119
Mauritian Cucumber Salad, *144*, 145
No Shrimp Curry, *106*, 107
Satini Cotomili (Cilantro Chutney), 218, *218*, 220
cinnamon, 22, *22*, 23
Carrot Juice, 205, *205*, 211
La Daube Banane, 174, *175*
Galangal Blood Orange Tea, *196*, 197, 198
Ginger Turmeric Tea, *196*, 197, 200
Grandma Bernice's Jamaican Pineapple-Skin Tea, 197, *197*, 202, *203*
Homemade Mauritian Curry Powder, 230, *230*, 231
Jamaican Chocolate Tea, 197, *197*, 201
Pilau Rice, *148*, 149
Tropical Pancakes with Pan-Grilled Pineapple, 58, *59*
cloves, 22, *22*, 23
Jamaican Sorrel, *188–89*, 189, *192*, 193
Pilau Rice, *148*, 149
coconut
Brioche Bread Pudding, *164*, 165
Coconut Banana Fritters, 160, *160–61*, *172*, 173
Gâteaux Koko, *176*, 177
Poudine Maïs, *180*, 181
Satini Coco (Coconut Chutney), 218, *218*, 222
Tropical Pancakes with Pan-Grilled Pineapple, 58, *59*
coconut flour, 160, *160–61*, *172*, 173
coconut milk and cream, 24. *See also* condensed milk, oat/coconut
Ackee and "No Saltfish," 42–43
La Daube Banane, 174, *175*
Green Banana Porridge, *40*, 41
Green Curry with Tofu Fish, Eggplant, and Rice Cakes, 75, *76*, 77
Haricots Rouges and Rice, 146, *147*
Homemade Coconut Condensed Milk, 228
Jamaican Chocolate Tea, 197, *197*, 201
One-Pot Pumpkin Soup, 102, *102*, 103
Tropical Pancakes with Pan-Grilled Pineapple, 58, *59*
Tropical Sea Moss Slammer, 189, *189*, 191
coconut oil, 24
coconut sugar, 24
Coconut Brown Sugar Rice Pudding, *64*, 65
Fried Bakes, *128*, 129
Homemade Coconut Condensed Milk, 228
Sticky Toffee Pudding, 182, *183*
coconut water
Tropical Charcoal Detox Smoothie Bowl, 52, *53*
Coleslaw, *82*, 83
condensed milk, oat/coconut, 41
Carrot Juice, 205, *205*, 211
Gâteaux Koko, *176*, 177
Homemade Coconut Condensed Milk, 228
Jamaican Guinness Punch, *188*, 189, 190
My Famous Three-Ingredient Mango Ice Cream, 178, *179*
condiments, 217–27, *218*
cookware, 29, 31
coriander seeds, 20, 22, *22*
Homemade Mauritian Curry Powder, 230, *230*, 231
corn
Bol Renversé, 72, *73*, 74, *74*
Grilled Jerk Corn on the Cob, *124*, 125
One-Pot Pumpkin Soup, 102, *102*, 103
cornmeal
Poudine Maïs, *180*, 181
cream. *See* coconut milk and cream; milk and cream, vegan
The Creamiest, Cheesiest Vegan Mac 'n' Cheese – Ever!, 159, 160, *161*
Creamy Cashew-Based Tzatziki, 108, 226
Creole Mauritians, 11, 12
Creole Rum Passion Cocktail, *188*, 189, 191
Crispy Onion Bhajis, *114–15*, 116, *117*
cucumber
Creamy Cashew-Based Tzatziki, 108, 226
Mauritian Cucumber Salad, *144*, 145
Mauritian Tropical Fruit Salad, 170, *171*
cumin, 20
Homemade Mauritian Curry Powder, 230, *230*, 231
curry leaves, 18, *18*, 20, 140
Fricasser Lentilles Noires, *138*, 139
Green Banana Rundown, 84, *85*
Green Curry with Tofu Fish, Eggplant, and Rice Cakes, 75, *76*, 77
Homemade Mauritian Curry Powder, 230, *230*, 231
Mauritian Butter Bean Soup, 101, 102, *102*
No Shrimp Curry, *106*, 107
Rougaille Pistache, 134, *135*
Rougaille Sauce (recipe), *132*, 133
Satini Coco, 218, *218*, 222
Tofu Vindaye, *86*, 87

curry powder
Jamaican Vegan Beef Puffs, 122, *123*
No Shrimp Curry, *106*, 107
cutting board, 29

D

dal. *See* lentils/dal; urad dal
dates
Date Candy Bar, 166, *167–69*
Mango Chile Lassi, *60*, 61
Sticky Toffee Pudding, 182, *183*
La Daube Banane (Spiced Sweet and Sticky Plantains), 174, *175*
dill
Creamy Cashew-Based Tzatziki, 108, 226

E

East London Kebab Shop Gyro, 108, *109*
Edgar's Vegan Goulash, *110*, 111
Effortless Homemade Chapatis (Indian Flatbread), *152*, 153
eggplant, 18, *18*
Green Curry with Tofu Fish, Eggplant, and Rice Cakes, 75, *76*, 77
eggs, vegan. *See also* tofu
Bol Renversé, 72, *73*, 74, *74*
Rougaille Dizef (Eggs in Tomato Sauce), *70*, 71
sourcing, 28
Eggy Seasoning Mix
recipe, 230, *230*, 232
Tropical Plantain and "Egg" Breakfast Sandwiches, 66, *67*
equipment, 29, *30*, 31

F

fennel seeds, 101
Homemade Mauritian Curry Powder, 230, *230*, 231
fenugreek, 20, 75, 77, 87, 101
Homemade Mauritian Curry Powder, 230, *230*, 231
fish sauce, vegan, 28
Ackee and "No Saltfish," 42–43
Bol Renversé, 72, *73*, 74, *74*
Green Curry with Tofu Fish, Eggplant, and Rice Cakes, 75, *76*, 77
Mine Frire, *78*, 79
fish seasoning mix
Ackee and "No Saltfish," 42–43
flours, specialty. *See also* rice flour
atta, *152*, 153
chickpea, *114–15*, 116, *117*
coconut, 160, *160–61*, *172*, 173
food coloring, *176*, 177
Fricasser Lentilles Noires (Mauritian Black Lentil Soup), *138*, 139
Fried Bakes, *128*, 129
Fried Plantains, 150, *151*

G

Galangal Blood Orange Tea, *196*, 197, 198
garam masala
Haricots Rouges and Rice, 146, *147*
Tofu Tikka Kebabs, 104, *105*
garlic, 18, *18*
Chile and Makrut Lime Garlic Bread, 158, 160, *160*
Jerk Dry Rub Seasoning, 229, 230, *230*
Piment Crazée (Mauritian Chile Garlic Paste), 218, *218*, 221
garlic chives
Mine Frire, *78*, 79
garlic paste
Fricasser Lentilles Noires, *138*, 139
No Shrimp Curry, *106*, 107
Satini Mangue Vert, 218, *218*, 223
garlic powder, 88, 95, 155
All-Purpose Seasoning, 230, *230*, 233
Eggy Seasoning Mix, 230, *230*, 232
Jerk Dry Rub Seasoning, 229, 230, *230*
Gâteau Piment (Chile Cakes), *114–15*, *118*, 119
Gâteaux Koko (Mauritian Coconut Macaroons), *176*, 177
ginger, 18, *18*, 23
Ackee and "No Saltfish," 42–43
Bol Renversé, 72, *73*, 74, *74*
Bouillon Cresson with Crispy Lion's Mane Mushrooms, 98, *99*
Carrot Juice, 205, *205*, 211
Ginger Turmeric Tea, *196*, 197, 200
Grandma Bernice's Jamaican Pineapple-Skin Tea, 197, *197*, 202, *203*
Green Banana Rundown, 84, *85*
Jamaican Sorrel, *188–89*, 189, *192*, 193
Lemon Zinger, *212*, 213, 214
Mine Frire, *78*, 79
Rougaille Sauce (recipe), *132*, 133
Satini Cotomili, 218, *218*, 220
Satini Mangue Vert, 218, *218*, 223
Scotch Bonnet Mango Hot Sauce, 218, *218*, *225*
Tamarind Sauce, 218, *218*, 219
Ugo Verde, 205, *205*, 210
Goji Berry Shot, *212–13*, 213, 215
golden syrup, 182, *183*
Grandma Bernice's Jamaican Pineapple-Skin Tea, 197, *197*, 202, *203*
granola
Breakfast Cereal Sea Moss Shake, 48, *49*
green bananas, 18, *18*
Green Banana Porridge, *40*, 41
Green Banana Rundown, 84, *85*
green beans
Touffer Haricots Verts à la Mauricienne, 100, 102, *102*
green chiles, 18, *18*
Gâteau Piment, *114–15*, *118*, 119
Mauritian Lentil Crepes, 92, *93*
Mine Frire, *78*, 79
One-Pot Pumpkin Soup, 102, *102*, 103
Piment Crazée (Mauritian Chile Garlic Paste), 218, *218*, 221
Rougaille Sauce (recipe), *132*, 133
Satini Coco, 218, *218*, 222
Satini Cotomili, 218, *218*, 220
Satini Mangue Vert, 218, *218*, 223
Vegetable Achard, *136*, 137
Green Curry with Tofu Fish, Eggplant, and Rice Cakes, 75, *76*, 77
green mango, 170
Mango Satini, 102, *102*, 160, *160*, 218, *218*, 224
Satini Mangue Vert (Green Mango Chutney), 218, *218*, 223
Grilled Jerk Corn on the Cob, *124*, 125
Guinness beer
Jamaican Guinness Punch, *188*, 189, 190

H

Haricots Rouges (Spiced Red Kidney Beans) and Rice, 146, *147*
hearts of palm
Ackee and "No Saltfish," 42–43
hibiscus (sorrel)
Jamaican Sorrel, *188–89*, 189, *192*, 193
Homemade Coconut Condensed Milk, 228
Homemade Idlis (Soft Rice Cakes), *76*, 77
Homemade Mauritian Curry Powder, 230, *230*, 231
honey, vegan, 150, *151*

I

ice cream, vegan, 173
Mauritian Aloudas (Rose and Mint Ice Cream Floats), *184*, 185
My Famous Three-Ingredient Mango Ice Cream, 178, *179*
ingredients, 25
homemade seasonings and condiments, 217–33
Jamaican, 23, 24
Mauritian, 19–20, 24
vegan tool kit, *26*, 27–28

J

Jamaica, 12, 15, 35, 113, 163
ingredients, 23, 24

Jamaican Avocado Toast with Fried Plantains, 62, *63*
Jamaican Cabbage and Bacon, 142, *143*
Jamaican Chocolate Tea, 197, *197*, 201
Jamaican Fried Dumplings, 44, *45*
Jamaican Guinness Punch, *188*, 189, 190
Jamaican "No Saltfish" Fritters, 36, *37*, 38, *39*
Jamaican Sorrel (Hibiscus Drink), *188–89*, 189, *192*, 193
Jamaican Vegan Beef Puffs, 122, *123*
jars, 31
jerk seasoning
  Grilled Jerk Corn on the Cob, *124*, 125
  Jerk Dry Rub Seasoning, 229, 230, *230*
  Jerk Mushroom Tacos, *82*, 83
juicer, 29

K

Kebab Shop Chili Sauce, 108, 227
kelp powder
  Ackee and "No Saltfish," 42–43
  Vegan Fish and Chips, *94*, 95–96, *97*
kids, 15–16
knives, 29

L

lemon
  Apple Cider Vinegar Shot, *212*, 213, 214
  Goji Berry Shot, *212–13*, 213, 215
  Grandma Bernice's Jamaican Pineapple-Skin Tea, 197, *197*, 202, *203*
  Lemon Zinger, *212*, 213, 214
  Piment Crazée, 218, *218*, 221
  Tamarind Lemonade, 194, *195*
lentils/dal, 20. *See also* urad dal
  Fricasser Lentilles Noires, *138*, 139
  Homemade Idlis, *76*, 77
  Mauritian Lentil Crepes, 92, *93*
lime, 225
  Chile and Makrut Lime Garlic Bread, 158, 160, *160*
  Sea Moss Watermelon Juice, *204*, 205, 207
  Ugo Verde, 205, *205*, 210
lion's mane mushrooms, 98, *99*
Lisou Touffé (Mauritian Sautéed Cabbage), 140
London, 12, 15, 108

M

maca root powder, 22, *22*
  Cacao, Sea Moss, and Maca Smoothie Bowl, *50*, 51
makrut lime
  Chile and Makrut Lime Garlic Bread, 158, 160, *160*
malta
  Carrot Juice, 205, *205*, 211
malt vinegar, 88, 90, 221
mango, 24, *25*. *See also* green mango
  Mango Chile Lassi, *60*, 61
  Mango Satini, 102, *102*, 160, *160*, 218, *218*, 224
  Mauritian Tropical Fruit Salad, 170, *171*
  My Famous Three-Ingredient Mango Ice Cream, 178, *179*
  Satini Mangue Vert (Green Mango Chutney), 218, *218*, 223
  Scotch Bonnet Mango Hot Sauce, 218, *218*, 225
  Tropical Sea Moss Slammer, 189, *189*, 191
Margose Frire (Stir-Fried Bitter Gourd), 156, *157*, 160, *160*
Mauritian Aloudas (Rose and Mint Ice Cream Floats), *184*, 185
Mauritian Butter Bean Soup, 101, 102, *102*
Mauritian Cucumber Salad, *144*, 145
Mauritian Gâteau Arouille (Taro Fritters), *114–15*, 120, *121*
Mauritian Lentil Crepes, 92, *93*
Mauritian Tropical Fruit Salad, 170, *171*
Mauritius, 11, 12, 15, 113, 163
  ingredients, 19–20, 24
mayonnaise, vegan
  Coleslaw, *82*, 83
  Tartar Sauce, *94*, 95–96, *97*
milk and cream, vegan. *See also* coconut milk; condensed milk, oat/coconut; oat milk
  Breakfast Cereal Sea Moss Shake, 48, *49*
  Brioche Bread Pudding, *164*, 165
  Carrot Juice, 205, *205*, 211
  The Creamiest, Cheesiest Vegan Mac 'n' Cheese – Ever!, 159, 160, *161*
  evaporated, 211
  Jamaican Guinness Punch, *188*, 189, 190
  Mango Chile Lassi, *60*, 61
  Mauritian Aloudas, *184*, 185
  Sticky Toffee Pudding, 182, *183*
Mine Frire (Mauritian Fried Noodles), *78*, 79
mint
  Satini Coco, 218, *218*, 222
mint syrup
  Mauritian Aloudas (Rose and Mint Ice Cream Floats), *184*, 185
mortar and pestle, 31
mushroom powder, 52, *53*
mushrooms
  Bol Renversé, 72, *73*, 74, *74*
  Bouillon Cresson with Crispy Lion's Mane Mushrooms, 98, *99*
  Jerk Mushroom Tacos, *82*, 83
  Vegan Fried Chicken, 88, *89*, 90, *91*
music/musicians, 11, 15, 16
mustard seeds, 20, 22, *22*, *86*, 87
My Famous Three-Ingredient Mango Ice Cream, 178, *179*

N

New York City, 16
noodles. *See* pasta and noodles
nori
  Ackee and "No Saltfish," 42–43
  Vegan Fish and Chips, *94*, 95–96, *97*
No Shrimp Curry, *106*, 107
nutmeg, 23, *82*, 83
  Carrot Juice, 205, *205*, 211
  La Daube Banane, 174, *175*
  Jamaican Chocolate Tea, 197, *197*, 201
  Tropical Pancakes with Pan-Grilled Pineapple, 58, *59*
nutritional yeast, 27
  The Creamiest, Cheesiest Vegan Mac 'n' Cheese – Ever!, 159, 160, *161*
  Eggy Seasoning Mix, 230, *230*, 232

O

oat milk, 28, 88, 90. *See also* condensed milk, oat/coconut
  Cacao, Sea Moss, and Maca Smoothie Bowl, *50*, 51
  Coconut Brown Sugar Rice Pudding, *64*, 65
  Green Banana Porridge, *40*, 41
  Poudine Maïs, *180*, 181
okra
  Spicy Baked Okra Fries, *154*, 155, 160, *160–61*
Old Bay seasoning
  Green Curry with Tofu Fish, Eggplant, and Rice Cakes, 75, *76*, 77
  Vegan Fried Chicken, 88, *89*, 90, *91*
One-Pot Pumpkin Soup, 102, *102*, 103
onion
  Crispy Onion Bhajis, *114–15*, 116, *117*
  Piment Crazée, 218, *218*, 221
  Vegetable Achard, *136*, 137
onion powder, 90, 155, 159
  All-Purpose Seasoning, 230, *230*, 233
  Eggy Seasoning Mix, 230, *230*, 232

onion powder (*cont.*)
Jerk Dry Rub Seasoning, 229, 230, *230*
orange
Galangal Blood Orange Tea, *196*, 197, 198
Grandma Bernice's Jamaican Pineapple-Skin Tea, 197, *197*, 202, *203*
Lemon Zinger, *212*, 213, 214
oregano, 233
oyster mushrooms, 27
Jerk Mushroom Tacos, *82*, 83
Vegan Fried Chicken, 88, *89*, 90, *91*
oyster sauce, vegan, 72
Mine Frire, *78*, 79

P

pancakes
Super Fluffy "Bacon" Pancakes, *54*, 55, *56–57*, 57
Tropical Pancakes with Pan-Grilled Pineapple, 58, *59*
pans, 29
paprika
All-Purpose Seasoning, 230, *230*, 233
Edgar's Vegan Goulash, *110*, 111
parsley
East London Kebab Shop Gyro, 108, *109*
Ugo Verde, 205, *205*, 210
passion fruit
Creole Rum Passion Cocktail, *188*, 189, 191
Passion Fruit Vinaigrette, *46*, 47
pasta and noodles
The Creamiest, Cheesiest Vegan Mac 'n' Cheese – Ever!, 159, 160, *161*
Mauritian Aloudas, *184*, 185
Mine Frire, *78*, 79
peanut butter
Date Candy Bar, 166, *167–69*
Rougaille Pistache (Mauritian Peanut Sauce), 134, *135*
peppers, hot. *See* chiles; Scotch bonnet peppers
Pickled Vegetables (Vegetable Achard), *136*, 137
pickles
Tartar Sauce, *94*, 95–96, *97*
Pilau Rice, *148*, 149
Piment Crazée (Mauritian Chile Garlic Paste), 218, *218*, 221
pimento berries
Green Banana Rundown, 84, *85*
pineapple
Grandma Bernice's Jamaican Pineapple-Skin Tea, 197, *197*, 202, *203*
Mauritian Tropical Fruit Salad, 170, *171*
Tropical Charcoal Detox Smoothie Bowl, 52, *53*
Tropical Pancakes with Pan-Grilled Pineapple, 58, *59*
Tropical Sea Moss Slammer, 189, *189*, 191
Ugo Verde, 205, *205*, 210
pita bread
East London Kebab Shop Gyro, 108, *109*
plantain, 18, *18*, 23
La Daube Banane (Spiced Sweet and Sticky Plantains), 174, *175*
Fried Plantains, 150, *151*
Jamaican Avocado Toast with Fried Plantains, 62, *63*
Plantain Breakfast Waffle, *46*, 47
Tropical Plantain and "Egg" Breakfast Sandwiches, 66, *67*
playlist, music, 16
polenta
Poudine Maïs (Polenta Pudding), *180*, 181
potatoes
Edgar's Vegan Goulash, *110*, 111
Lisou Touffé, 140
Touffer Haricots Verts à la Mauricienne, 100, 102, *102*
Vegan Fish and Chips, *94*, 95–96, *97*
Poudine Maïs (Polenta Pudding), *180*, 181
pretzels
Date Candy Bar, 166, *167–69*
puff pastry
Jamaican Vegan Beef Puffs, 122, *123*
pumpkin
One-Pot Pumpkin Soup, 102, *102*, 103

R

raisins, 181
Brioche Bread Pudding, *164*, 165
Rastafarians, 12
red chiles. *See* chiles
rice
Bol Renversé, 72, *73*, 74, *74*
Bouillon Cresson with Crispy Lion's Mane Mushrooms, 98, *99*
Coconut Brown Sugar Rice Pudding, *64*, 65
Haricots Rouges and Rice, 146, *147*
Homemade Idlis, *76*, *77*
Pilau Rice, *148*, 149
rice cakes
Green Curry with Tofu Fish, Eggplant, and Rice Cakes, 75, *76*, *77*
recipe, *76*, *77*
rice flour, 95
Crispy Onion Bhajis, *114–15*, 116, *117*
Homemade Idlis, *76*, *77*
Roasted and Fried Breadfruit Wedges, 126, *127*
Rookwood, Charlise, *10*, *14*, *17*, *32*, *34*, *68*, *112*, *128*, *130*, *162*, *186*, *199*, *208–9*, *216*
background, 11–16
cooking show, 11, 108, 159, 166
music, 11, 15
Rookwood, Whylie, 9, 15, *16*, 234–35
rose syrup
Mauritian Aloudas (Rose and Mint Ice Cream Floats), *184*, 185
Rougaille Pistache (Mauritian Peanut Sauce), 134, *135*
Rougaille Sauce (Tomato Sauce)
Bouillon Cresson with Crispy Lion's Mane Mushrooms, 98, *99*
recipe, *132*, 133
Rougaille Dizef, *70*, 71
Rougaille Saucisse, 80, *81*
rum
Creole Rum Passion Cocktail, *188*, 189, 191

S

salt, 22, *22*
Chili Salt, 170, *171*
Himalayan black, 27, 104, 232
Satini Coco (Coconut Chutney), 218, *218*, 222
Satini Cotomili (Cilantro Chutney), 218, *218*, 220
Satini Mangue Vert (Green Mango Chutney), 218, *218*, 223
sausages, vegan
Rougaille Saucisse (Sausages in Tomato Sauce), 80, *81*
scallions, 18, *18*
Scotch bonnet peppers, 18, *18*, 23
Callaloo Sauté, *45*, 141
Green Banana Rundown, 84, *85*
Jamaican "No Saltfish" Fritters, 36, *37*, 38, *39*
Jerk Mushroom Tacos, *82*, 83
Plantain Breakfast Waffle, *46*, 47
Scotch Bonnet Mango Hot Sauce, 218, *218*, 225
sea moss, 22, *22*, 23, 28
Breakfast Cereal Sea Moss Shake, 48, *49*
Cacao, Sea Moss, and Maca Smoothie Bowl, *50*, 51
Sea Moss Watermelon Juice, *204*, 205, 207
Tropical Sea Moss Slammer, 189, *189*, 191
seasonings. *See* ingredients; spices; *specific seasonings*
Seventh-day Adventist, 12
shiitake mushrooms, 72, *73*
shrimp, vegan, 27
No Shrimp Curry, *106*, 107
shrimp paste, vegan
Green Curry with Tofu Fish,

Eggplant, and Rice Cakes, 75, *76*, 77
sorrel (hibiscus)
Jamaican Sorrel, *188–89*, 189, *192*, 193
sources, for vegan ingredients, 27–28
soy sauce, 28, 72
spices. *See also specific spices*
blends, 229–33
essential, 19–20, *22*, 23
tempering, 20, *21*
Spicy Baked Okra Fries, *154*, 155, 160, *160–61*
spinach
Green Curry with Tofu Fish, Eggplant, and Rice Cakes, 75, *76*, 77
Tropical Charcoal Detox Smoothie Bowl, 52, *53*
split lentils. *See* lentils/dal
split peas
Gâteau Piment, *114–15*, *118*, 119
star anise
Ginger Turmeric Tea, *196*, 197, 200
Sticky Toffee Pudding, 182, *183*
strainers, 31
substitutes, plant-based, 27–28
sugar. *See* coconut sugar
sunflower seed butter
Breakfast Cereal Sea Moss Shake, 48, *49*
Super Fluffy "Bacon" Pancakes, *54*, 55, *56–57*, 57
sweetened condensed milk. *See* condensed coconut milk
Sweet Potato Juice, *204*, 205, 206

T

tamarind, 18, *18*, 24–25
Satini Coco, 218, *218*, 222
Tamarind Drizzle, 170, *171*
Tamarind Lemonade, 194, *195*
Tamarind Sauce, 218, *218*, 219
taro
Mauritian Gâteau Arouille, *114–15*, 120, *121*
Tartar Sauce, *94*, 95–96, *97*
tempering spices, 20, *21*
Thai basil, 18, *18*
thyme, 18, *18*, 23, 42–43, 75, 142
All-Purpose Seasoning, 230, *230*, 233
Rougaille Pistache, 134, *135*
tofu
Green Curry with Tofu Fish, Eggplant, and Rice Cakes, 75, *76*, 77
Tofu Tikka Kebabs, 104, *105*
Tofu Vindaye, *86*, 87
Tropical Plantain and "Egg" Breakfast Sandwiches, 66, *67*
tomato
Ackee and "No Saltfish," 42–43
Callaloo Sauté, *45*, 141
Fricasser Lentilles Noires, *138*, 139
Green Banana Rundown, 84, *85*
Haricots Rouges and Rice, 146, *147*
Jamaican Cabbage and Bacon, 142, *143*
Jamaican "No Saltfish" Fritters, 36, *37*, 38, *39*
Kebab Shop Chili Sauce, 108, 227
Lisou Touffé, 140
Mauritian Butter Bean Soup, 101, 102, *102*
No Shrimp Curry, *106*, 107
Rougaille Pistache, 134, *135*
Rougaille Sauce (recipe), *132*, 133
Satini Cotomili, 218, *218*, 220
tomato paste/sauce, 42–43. *See also* Rougaille Sauce
Edgar's Vegan Goulash, *110*, 111
Haricots Rouges and Rice, 146, *147*
Jamaican Vegan Beef Puffs, 122, *123*
Kebab Shop Chili Sauce, 108, 227
Tofu Tikka Kebabs, 104, *105*
tools, 29, *30*, 31
Touffer Haricots Verts à la Mauricienne (Sautéed French Beans with Potatoes), 100, 102, *102*
Tropical Charcoal Detox Smoothie Bowl, 52, *53*
Tropical Pancakes with Pan-Grilled Pineapple, 58, *59*
Tropical Plantain and "Egg" Breakfast Sandwiches, 66, *67*
Tropical Sea Moss Slammer, 189, *189*, 191
turmeric, 20, 22, *22*
Apple Cider Vinegar Shot, *212*, 213, 214
black pepper and, benefits of, 198
Eggy Seasoning Mix, 230, *230*, 232
Ginger Turmeric Tea, *196*, 197, 200
Grandma Bernice's Jamaican Pineapple-Skin Tea, 197, *197*, 202, *203*
Homemade Mauritian Curry Powder, 230, *230*, 231
Lemon Zinger, *212*, 213, 214
Mango Chile Lassi, *60*, 61
Tofu Vindaye, *86*, 87
tzatziki, 108, 226

U

Ugo Verde (Green Juice), 205, *205*, 210
urad dal, 222
Homemade Idlis, *76*, *77*

V

vanilla, 41, 55, 65, 177, 181, 182, 190, 211
Carrot Juice, 205, *205*, 211
La Daube Banane, 174, *175*
Tropical Pancakes with Pan-Grilled Pineapple, 58, *59*
vanilla-based rum
Creole Rum Passion Cocktail, *188*, 189, 191
Vegan Fish and Chips, *94*, 95–96, *97*
Vegan Fried Chicken, 88, *89*, 90, *91*
Vegan Soulicious (social media platform), 11
vegan tool kit (ingredients), *26*, 27–28
Vegetable Achard (Pickled Vegetables), *136*, 137

W

waffles
maker, *30*, 31
Plantain Breakfast Waffle, *46*, 47
watercress
Bouillon Cresson (Watercress Broth) with Crispy Lion's Mane Mushrooms, 98, *99*
watermelon
Sea Moss Watermelon Juice, *204*, 205, 207
whipping cream, vegan, 178, *179*
wok, 31

Y

yams
One-Pot Pumpkin Soup, 102, *102*, 103
yellow split peas
Gâteau Piment, *114–15*, *118*, 119
yogurt, dairy-free
Mango Chile Lassi, *60*, 61
Tofu Tikka Kebabs, 104, *105*

Editor: Laura Dozier
Designer: Annie Marino
Design Manager: Danielle Youngsmith
Managing Editor: Annalea Manalili
Production Manager: Kathleen Gaffney

Library of Congress Control Number: 2024942504

ISBN: 978-1-4197-7570-3
eISBN: 979-8-88707-349-1

Printed and bound in China
10 9 8 7 6 5 4 3 2 1

ABRAMS The Art of Books
195 Broadway, New York, NY 10007
abramsbooks.com